PRAYERTIME
Cycle B

Faith-Sharing Reflections on the Sunday Gospels

Robert Heyer, Editor

U.K. editors
Stuart Wilson, Joe Kennedy &
Lindsey Russell

Pau
Rita
Biag
Jean Marie Hiesberger
Mary Lou Verla
Kathy Hendricks

GW00584887

RENEW International
Plainfield, New Jersey

NIHIL OBSTAT
For the United States:
Reverend Lawrence E. Frizzell, D.Phil.
Archdiocese of Newark Theological Commission
Censor Librorum

For the United Kingdom:
Reverend Terence McGuckin, BA, STL Mlitt, DD

IMPRIMATUR
Most Reverend Paul G. Bootkoski, D.D., V.G.
Administrator, Archdiocese of Newark

US edition:
Library of Congress Catalog Card Number: 2001119347
Main entry under title
PRAYERTIME, Cycle B
cm.
ISBN 1-930978-03-0   (paper, vol. 2)
1. Church year meditations. 2. Prayer groups-Catholic Church. 3. Catholic Church
Custom and practices. 4. Common lectionary-Meditations. I. Heyer, Robert J.,
editor, 1933- .

Published by the Diocese of Westminster, UK on behalf of RENEW International,
1232 George Street, Plainfield, NJ 07062-1717
Web site: www.renewintl.org Phone: +01 908-769-5400

Printed and bound in the U.K. by Livesey Limited

Contents

Acknowledgments

The editor would like to thank
Msgr Tom Kleissler
Mary C. McGuinness, OP
Katherine Andrews, Melissa Cavallo and Julie Jones

Authors
Paul Covino
Rita Ferrone
Biagio Mazza
Jean Marie Hiesberger
Mary Lou Verla
Kathy Hendricks

Consultants
Fathers John Russell, O. Carm., S.T.D. and James M. Cafone, S.T.D.
Those who carefully read the text and gave very helpful thoughts, especially Roberta Hazelbaker.
Small Christian community members from various dioceses who piloted sessions and offered their valuable comments.

U.K Acknowledgments

Editing the text
Fr Christopher Bedford
Sr Amadeus Bulger, CJ
Joe Kennedy
Fr Stuart Wilson

Music Resources
Chris Castell

i

Foreword

The idea for this series of books comes from so many of you. Many of our readers are using this book because they have been part of the Diocese of Westminster programme of Pastoral and Spiritual Renewal which we named *"At Your Word, Lord"*. For five Seasons of six weeks they grew in the knowledge of faith sharing in small Christian communities – and they didn't want to give it up. Now the majority of our parishes have small Christian communities which meet regularly. It is for these groups that we, in partnership with RENEW International, produced this UK version of *PRAYERTIME* Cycle B.

PRAYERTIME B is not limited to the Diocese of Westminster. It can be used anywhere and by anyone. As long as you are committed to the belief that God can and will speak to you through the Scriptures, through the Tradition of the Church and through the experience of every Christian then this book is for you. Remember too that the book is your servant and not your master. You are allowed to adapt, to slow down, to think different thoughts to respond to different questions. *PRAYERTIME* B is a catalyst and a guide to set you going on an exciting journey which you will not regret.

If this book is not your master – then please do see it as a sympathetic teacher and listen to some of its requests. Occasionally a group will report that they have "stalled" or "become stale". Inevitably this is because they have failed to do the one thing that is vital. They have failed to address the whole area of making a response at the end of each week. Small Christian communities are fascinating because they move those who participate in them from comfort to challenge. The challenge is in the response but it all too easy to spend time talking and sharing without allowing sufficient time to make the response to God. Having heard God's word what must I do? It is an easy question to ask but not so easy to answer. The measure of your commitment will be experienced in the answer you make each week.

May God bless you as you use this book and grow in fellowship with each other and with Him.

Stuart Wilson, Joe Kennedy & Lindsey Russell
Joint UK Editors
(on behalf of the *At Your Word, Lord* Team)

Introduction

PRAYERTIME, Cycle B offers a resource for faith sharing based on Scripture. Using the Sunday gospel of Cycle B as the focus, meaningful reflections, focused faith-sharing questions, related actions for consideration, and prayers on each Sunday reading are proposed as sources for nourishment, renewal, and inspiration.

Each group using *PRAYERTIME* needs to have a prayer leader who is familiar with the service and process. This leader should obtain the Sunday gospel of the appropriate service. A liturgical calendar is included in the back of the book to assist both leaders and participants. Also, the leader should prepare the copies of the music selection if this is chosen as the opening prayer. Appointing someone to lead the song might be helpful. Suggested songs are listed, but groups should feel free to choose their own songs. A list of music resources can be found in the back of the book.

The service is designed to be flexible in the time required. Depending upon the size and purpose of the gathering, the process could take from ten or fifteen minutes to thirty or ninety minutes. If the meeting is the regular staff meeting or parish pastoral council meeting, the process would be shorter. If it is a seasonal small Christian community meeting, the process would be longer.

The leader is encouraged to be creative in preparing an appropriate setting for sharing and prayer, eliminating distractions as much as possible.

Prayer Service Outline

At the first meeting or whenever new participants attend, all are invited to introduce themselves and share why they came.

At other times, this time might be used for sharing the experiences that resulted from specific action decisions from the previous meeting.

Invitation to Pray

The leader brings the group together and allows a few moments for appreciating God's presence.

The leader may begin with the suggested song or use the alternative collect prayer from the Sunday liturgy, prepare another brief prayer, invite a participant to pray, or use the following suggested prayer.

Loving God and Father, we ask your blessing upon our gathering. Open our minds and hearts to hear your Word and to act upon it. Give us the love and compassion of Jesus and the enlightenment of your Holy Spirit as we seek your will. We make our prayer through Jesus and the Holy Spirit who live in love with you. Amen

After the song or prayer, the Scripture reading is proclaimed. This means it has been prepared. The leader should foresee this and select a good reader who will prepare. If necessary for understanding, the reader might give the context of the Scripture reading in a sentence or two, so that all may appreciate the meaning of this gospel.

After the reading, the leader invites everyone to take a few moments to savor a word or feeling or question that arises in each person as he or she listens to the reading. The leader then asks those who wish to share this aloud.

Invitation to Reflect

The leader asks someone to read aloud the commentary or have all read it thoughtfully to themselves. Each person then shares his or her response to the Scripture. The questions may provide guides for this. The focus centres on how one experiences the action of God's Word in daily life.

Invitation to Group Sharing

After this reflection/sharing, the leader continues the group sharing by asking the first reflection question.

Each person should then share his or her response to the reflection and questions. The leader needs to bring each person gently into the sharing and not allow one person to dominate.

Invitation to Act

The leader decides the appropriate conclusion time to this sharing and moves on to talk about choosing a specific action. Each may choose an individual action or the group may want to do a common action. The primary consideration should be in determining a specific action (group or individual) that flows from the sharing. The actions listed are secondary suggestions.

When choosing individual actions, the leader will ask the members to share their decision with the group. When choosing a group action, the leader will guide the group in determining who will take responsibility for different aspects of the action.

Ministerial communities or committees may decide their tasks at hand are their responses. However, the task at hand need not be their only response. The Word always renews and challenges us.

At the beginning of the next session with this same group, the leader should begin by inviting people to share briefly how they carried out their action responses.

Invitation to Closing Prayer

The sharing is concluded with prayer.

The leader or someone he or she invites is responsible for the closing prayer. Each service has a closing prayer; however, the leader or participants may want to add or choose their own closing prayer.

Small Group Process

Small group/community sessions are a very important part of the parish's spiritual growth and development process. These small gatherings provide valuable opportunities for us, the people of God, to share our faith, to listen more closely to the Holy Spirit, and to witness that God has called us, and continues to touch us and heal us as individuals, families, neighbours, and parishioners.

Understanding and respecting the ways adults learn is an essential part of small faith-sharing groups. It is important that the atmosphere be comfortable, warm, and friendly. Ambiguity and differences of opinion are to be expected. Each person is given the opportunity to express feelings and thoughts, examined in light of the rich scriptural tradition of our faith. Being accepted and listened to are essential ingredients of a good faith-sharing experience. There should be a true desire to listen to another's experience. A sense of humour is always helpful!

The leader/facilitator is the person who has the responsibility for guiding the group through the faith sharing and prayers (or assigning them to one of the members) of the small group session. Leaders of the small groups must be well-trained for the task. By demonstrating charity and flexibility, a facilitator can effectively help the group to stay on the topic, gently include hesitant members, and develop a warm, accepting, open climate, and group cohesiveness.

Leaders do not provide preambles or prologues to questions; they do not frighten, shame, or argue with participants by word, gesture, expression, voice tone, or note taking. Participants may have questions about specific elements of our faith. Rather than trying to answer all questions, the facilitator may refer the questions to the pastor or parish staff to gain answers about our faith.

A leader listens carefully to the participants and asks questions only when necessary to keep the discussion moving or keep it on focus. The leader needs to be prepared by understanding beforehand the questions and the background provided in the text. However, the leader need never be a slave to a set of questions or text, but should be able to adapt to what is needed for the sharing as it moves along.

When two or more Christians share faith, we are assured that Christ is in our midst and that the life of God and gifts of the Spirit of God are at work in us (see Matthew 18:20). Through the small group/community sessions, we are in a very vital way opening ourselves to the Spirit's working in us and through us.

Faith-Sharing Principles and Guidelines

In an effort to keep your group/community consistent with its purpose, we offer the following Faith-Sharing Principles and Guidelines:

Theological Principles

- **Each person is led by God on his or her personal spiritual journey. This happens in the context of the Church.**

- **Faith sharing refers to shared reflections on the action of God in one's life experience** as related to Scripture and the Church's faith. Faith sharing is not necessarily discussion, problem solving, or Scripture study. The purpose is an encounter between a person in the concrete circumstances of one's life and the Word of God that leads to a conversion of heart.

- **Faith sharing is meant to serve our union with Christ, his Church, and with one another.** With the help of God's Spirit, we contribute vitality to the whole Church. We receive authoritative guidance from the Church's leadership. We are nurtured in the sacramental life. We are supported by a community of believers for our mission in the world.

- **The entire faith-sharing process is seen as prayer,** that is, listening to the Word of God as broken open by others' experiences.

Small Group Guidelines

- **Constant attention to respect, honesty, and openness for each person will assist the group or community's growth.**

- **Each person shares on the level on which he or she feels comfortable.**

- **Silence is a vital part of the total process of faith sharing.** Participants are given time to reflect before any sharing begins, and a period of comfortable silence might occur between individual sharings.

- Persons are encouraged to wait to share a second time until others who wish to do so have contributed.

- The entire group is responsible for participating and faith sharing.

- Confidentiality is essential, allowing each person to share honestly.

- Reaching beyond the group in action and response is essential for the growth of individuals, the groups, and the Church.

Advent Season

First Sunday of Advent

Hope and Vigilance

Invitation to Pray

Pause for a few moments of silence and enter more deeply into the presence of God.

> *Song*: "O Jesus Christ, Remember,"
> Edward Caswall

> *Proclaim the gospel:* Mark 13:33-37
> Be Watchful!

Take a few minutes to savour a word, a phrase, a question, or a feeling that rises up in you. Reflect on this quietly or share it aloud. (The other Scripture readings of the day are Isaiah 63:16b-17, 19b; 64:2-7 and 1 Corinthians 1:3-9.)

Invitation to Reflect on the Gospel

There is a temptation to go through life waiting for some special, life-altering event to take place, whether it arrives by mail in a sudden, unexpected, climactic experience or in the arrival of a new, meaningful person on the scene. It can be a bit like waiting for the magical moment of winning the lottery.

We want to 'be watchful' in avoiding sinfulness or pre-occupation with unnecessary distractions that take our focus away from Christ. The Advent call expressed in today's gospel to "Be watchful! Be alert!" (Mark 13:33), must be more than a passive waiting. Active watchfulness challenges us to put our spiritual lives in order. It challenges us to have Christ be primary in our lives over all other pursuits, ambitions, or involvements.

Advent is a time for prayerful reflection, a time to be particularly alert to the promptings of God's grace. In what specific ways are we being called to change our lives? It is a time for generous good works in which our kindness and care for others displace excessive self-absorption and concern. Openheartedness, through engagement in good works, creates room for Christ's vital presence.

Too passive a waiting for the coming of Christ may find Christmas coming and going with little change in our lives. Active alertness and receptivity to the coming of Christ bring fulfilment of the promise: "I came so that they might have life and have it more abundantly" (John 10:10).

Invitation to Group Sharing

1. In what ways is God's grace urging me to a more conscious awareness of the presence of Christ and a deeper relationship with him?

2. How am I being called to make this Advent different from past Advents?

3. What place will prayer play in my Advent preparations?

Invitation to Act

Determine a specific action (individual or group) that flows from your sharing. This should be your primary consideration. When choosing an individual action, determine what you will do and share it with the group. When choosing a group action, determine who will take responsibility for different aspects of the action. The following are secondary suggestions:

1. Set aside a certain amount of time each day this Advent for prayer.

2. Make an Advent wreath and begin each meal during the season by lighting the appropriate number of candles and saying grace before eating. If you need some direction for your Advent prayer, see what materials are available from your parish or from a local Catholic bookshop.

3. If you have children (or grandchildren who live nearby), spend time with them during the often busy days and weeks before Christmas. Though they may not say it, children want your time even more than they want the Christmas gifts you're buying for them.

4. If you don't already have some, develop customs or traditions for Advent that include sharing with others who may not have been remembered or who are in more need than yourself.

5. Set up the stable from a nativity set and add a piece of straw to the manger each time a member of the household does a good work. By building up the place where the figure of the Christ Child will rest come Christmas Day, children and adults alike learn about preparing for the Lord by living out the gospel's call to love and service of others.

Invitation to Closing Prayer

Give thanks to God (aloud or silently) for insights gained, for desires awakened, for directions clarified, for the gift of one another's openness and sensitivity. Conclude with the following:

Leader God of all times, you alone know the time
     when Christ will return in glory.
     We thank you for bringing us together today
     around your Word.

     Set our hearts this Advent on using well
     the time you have given us on earth.
     Keep us alert to your presence
     in those around us, and fill us with hope
     as we strive to live in your reign.
     We ask this through Christ our Lord.

All   Amen

Leader Come, Lord Jesus!

All   Come, Lord Jesus!

Second Sunday of Advent

Patience and Forgiveness

Invitation to Pray

Pause for a few moments of silence and enter more deeply into the presence of God.

> ***Song:*** "On Jordan's Bank," Charles Coffin,
> tr. John Chandler

> ***Proclaim the gospel:*** Mark 1:1-8
> Make Straight the Paths of
> the Lord

Take a few minutes to savour a word, a phrase, a question, or a feeling that rises up in you. Reflect on this quietly or share it aloud. (The other Scripture readings of the day are Isaiah 40:1-5, 9-11 and 2 Peter 3:8-14.)

Invitation to Reflect on the Gospel

With clothing of camel's hair and a diet of locusts and wild honey, John the Baptist is certainly one of the more colourful characters in the Bible! This gospel opens with a declaration of Jesus as the Son of God and then promptly introduces John as the messenger who points to Jesus. John's method of preparing for Jesus was as unreserved as his appearance. He called people to repent, acknowledge their sins, and undergo baptism for forgiveness.

Unlike Lent, Advent is not primarily a penitential season. It does, however, invite us to acknowledge what in our lives, as individuals and as Christian communities, stands in the way of

God's reign. Unlike John the Baptist, we do not look forward to Christ's first coming among us, but rather to his coming to us anew each day and to his return in glory at the end of time, when God's reign will be fulfilled. John's call is nevertheless still valid – repentance and forgiveness are essential for those who would prepare the way of the Lord.

Our journey through Advent also teaches us another value needed by those who await the fulfillment of God's reign, and that is patience. Like the child struggling to resist the temptation to unwrap presents under the tree before Christmas arrives, we sometimes find ourselves wanting to "get through" Advent and get to Christmas. We want Christmas and we want it now! So it is with the glory of God's reign. We naturally want to enjoy it fully here and now, but Advent feeds us the wild honey of joyful expectation, reminding us that the reign of God is already being experienced but not yet complete.

Invitation to Group Sharing

1. What things try my patience? How do I ask God to help me? What might God be telling me about my response to situations that try my patience?

2. What in me needs to be forgiven? Whom do I need to forgive? How can I make forgiveness real in my life this Advent, as a means of preparing the way of the Lord?

3. Where are forgiveness and reconciliation necessary within our parish? Are we part of a group that needs to seek forgiveness and reconciliation with other parish groups? How might we go about doing this?

Invitation to Act

Determine a specific action (individual or group) that flows from your sharing. This should be your primary consideration. When choosing an individual action, determine what you will do and share it with the group. When choosing a group action, determine who will take responsibility for different aspects of the action. The following are secondary suggestions:

1. Celebrate forgiveness by participating in any penance services that may be planned in your parish this Advent. Check with the priest or liturgy committee to see if your small community might be able to assist at the service as greeters or by hosting a reception after the service.

2. Reach out in forgiveness and reconciliation to groups in the parish with whom you may have had some conflict.

3. In their journey toward Christian initiation, catechumens are living witnesses to the role of patience, reminding us that true conversion happens over time. If you don't know the catechumens in your parish, make Advent the time to introduce yourself to them. Remember them in your prayers. Participate in any rites that celebrate the stages of their initiation. Consider offering to serve as a sponsor for a catechumen.

Invitation to Closing Prayer

Give thanks to God (aloud or silently) for insights gained, for desires awakened, for directions clarified, for the gift of one another's openness and sensitivity. Conclude with the following:

Leader   God of the prophets, you sent John to prepare
the way for Christ through his baptism
of repentance for the forgiveness of sins.
Inspire us to prepare the way
for Christ's return in glory
by reaching out in forgiveness
and patiently living out the gospel.
We ask this through Christ our Lord.

All   Amen

Leader   Come, Lord Jesus!

All   Come, Lord Jesus!

Third Sunday of Advent

Peace and Justice

Invitation to Pray

Pause for a few moments of silence and enter more deeply into the presence of God.

> ***Song:*** "O Come, O Come, Emmanuel," verses 1-4,
> tr. John M. Neale

> ***Proclaim the gospel:*** John 1:6-8, 19-28
> There is One Among You Whom
> You Do Not Recognise

Take a few minutes to savour a word, a phrase, a question, or a feeling that rises up in you. Reflect on this quietly or share it aloud. (The other Scripture readings of the day are Isaiah 61:1-2a, 10-11 and 1 Thessalonians 5:16-24.)

Invitation to Reflect on the Gospel

Have you ever heard the expression that someone has a "messiah complex"? Usually, it means that the person believes or acts like he or she is capable of saving the world or at least solving all the problems of a particular group. Based on today's gospel, John the Baptist seemed to have every right to have a messiah complex. Priests, Levites, and Pharisees all ask him what many Jews were wondering: "Who are you?... Are you Elijah?... Are you the Prophet?" (John 1:19-21). John's response to the questions is adamant: "I am not the Messiah... I am not [Elijah]," but rather "I am 'the voice of one crying out in the desert, "Make straight the way of the Lord"'" (John 1:20-21, 23). John denies any special role for himself and instead portrays himself as pointing toward "the one who is coming after me" (John 1:27).

John models the kind of attitude and behaviour that each individual Christian and each Christian community are called to imitate. All that we do is meant to point to Christ and to direct others to Christ, not to call attention to ourselves or to heighten our own importance. We practice this when we reach beyond ourselves to help others live life to the fullest. Models of this kind of selfless love are still found amidst the often-overwhelming evils of our world. They are found among parents, spouses, friends, colleagues, priests and religious, public officials, and those who transcend their own self-importance so that others might move forward. They include those whose charity and work for justice "bring glad tidings to the lowly [and] …heal the brokenhearted" (see Isaiah 61:1, which is this Sunday's first reading). They illuminate our world as the Christmas lights illuminate the darkness of December nights. May we be numbered among them!

Invitation to Group Sharing

1. Who are the people who have allowed their self-importance to recede so I might grow and develop into the person God is calling me to be? How can I thank or acknowledge them?

2. In what ways do my attitude and actions point to Jesus Christ? In what ways do they point to me or try to call attention to my own importance?

3. How do my actions as a Christian and our actions as a Christian community "bring glad tidings to the lowly, [and] …heal the brokenhearted" (Isaiah 61:1)? How are my acts of charity during the holidays connected to my work for justice all year long?

Invitation to Act

Determine a specific action (individual or group) that flows from your sharing. This should be your primary consideration. When choosing an individual action, determine what you will do and share it with the group. When choosing a group action, determine who will take responsibility for different aspects of the action. The following are secondary suggestions:

1. Remember that any ministry or service you do is intended to help people experience the loving presence of Jesus Christ. If others thank or praise you for your service, be grateful for their appreciation and rejoice that the Lord has worked through you.

2. The second reading for this Sunday speaks of "the God of peace" (1 Thessalonians 5:23), yet peace is often overshadowed by stress in the days before Christmas. Help alleviate some of this stress for others by organizing a weekend afternoon of activities for children at the church or in the neighbourhood, so that parents can take care of Christmas preparations, or by offering to help a housebound person do the same.

3. Some of the people who receive our charity during the holiday season cannot break out of poverty because of inadequate education or training. Contact those responsible for pastoral affairs in your Diocese to see how your group or parish might be able to assist someone to receive the education or training necessary for a higher paying job, or perhaps help a person who doesn't yet have a job.

Invitation to Closing Prayer

Give thanks to God (aloud or silently) for insights gained, for desires awakened, for directions clarified, for the gift of one another's openness and sensitivity. Conclude with the following:

Leader   God of justice and peace, your servant John
testified to the light
that came into the world's darkness
in Jesus Christ the Lord.
God, our Father, may our charity to the poor
and our work for justice for all people
make straight the way that leads to you.
We ask this through Christ our Lord
and in the power of the Holy Spirit.

All   Amen

Leader   Come, Lord Jesus!

All   Come, Lord Jesus!

Fourth Sunday of Advent

Mary as Model Disciple

Invitation to Pray

Pause for a few moments of silence and enter more deeply into the presence of God.

> ***Song:*** "O Come, O Come, Emmanuel," verses 3-7,
> tr. John M. Neale

> ***Proclaim the gospel:*** Luke 1:26-38
> Behold, You Will Conceive in Your
> Womb and Bear a Son

Take a few minutes to savour a word, a phrase, a question, or a feeling that rises up in you. Reflect on this quietly or share it aloud. (The other Scripture readings of the day are 2 Samuel 7:1-5, 8b-12, 14a, 16 and Romans 16:25-27.)

Invitation to Reflect on the Gospel

"How can this be?" It's a perfectly normal reaction when we're faced with something that doesn't seem to make sense. It was certainly an understandable reaction from Mary in this gospel. An ordinary, humble Jewish girl, she is visited by an angel who tells her she will conceive a son without benefit of a husband, and this child will be the Son of God, the Messiah her people have longed for. How can this be, indeed!

What follows Mary's initial reaction, though, is what elevates her to the status of model disciple. She doesn't try to bargain with the angel ("Just let me get married first, and then I'll be happy to be the mother of God!"), nor does she resort to what we might call a "take charge attitude" ("If I'm going to give birth to the Son of God, then we've got some planning to do!"). Rather, her response is one of complete acceptance of God's will: "I am the handmaid of the Lord. May it be done to me according to your word" (Luke 1:38). Mary's "yes" with no conditions finds a parallel years later in her Son's acceptance of God's will on the night before his crucifixion: "not my will but yours be done" (Luke 22:42). Her unconditional "yes" reveals her discipleship.

In the Christmas film "Miracle on 34th Street," a single mother and her daughter come to see that faith involves believing in something invisible to the human eye. As wonderful as that film is, it pales in comparison to the story of faith in today's gospel. Despite any assurances of what the future will hold, Mary places her complete trust in God and does what God asks. This is the model we are called to emulate. God does not give us a script for our lives so that we might see what lies ahead. Jesus' birth, death, and Resurrection did not mean that we would never face suffering or difficulty. God simply promises never to abandon us, no matter what we face in life. God's power, which overshadowed Mary, will also come upon us in the joys and challenges we encounter. That's the miracle for those who trust in God.

Invitation to Group Sharing

1. In what ways do I see Mary as a disciple of Christ? As a model of Christian discipleship?

2. Am I alert and open to God's call? How is God calling me to be a disciple in my life? What holds me back from accepting what God is asking?

3. How much do I trust God? Do I believe that God, whose power overshadowed Mary, will be there for me in the joys and challenges of my life?

4. How might we embrace Mary's model of discipleship and let it influence our own lives? Our family life?

Invitation to Act

Determine a specific action (individual or group) that flows from your sharing. This should be your primary consideration. When choosing an individual action, determine what you will do and share it with the group. When choosing a group action, determine who will take responsibility for different aspects of the action. The following are secondary suggestions:

1. Recall times in your life when you consciously put your trust in God and were aware that God was present to you and watching over you. Thank God for those times. Thank the people who were a sign of God's presence to you.

2. Read more about Mary and her role in our faith. Study the publication produced by a group of Anglican and Roman Catholic theologians entitled *Mary: Grace and Hope in Christ* to see what unites and also what separates Christians in their understanding of the role of Mary. You may also check the Web site www.esbvm.org.uk which will give you information about the Ecumenical Society of the Blessed Virgin Mary which promotes ecumenical study of and devotion to Mary, the Mother of God.

3. The Solemnity of Mary, Mother of God is celebrated on 1st January. Check with the priest or liturgy committee to see if your small community might be able to assist at the Mass as welcomers or by hosting a reception after the Mass to honour Mary and celebrate the New Year.

Invitation to Closing Prayer

Give thanks to God (aloud or silently) for insights gained, for desires awakened, for directions clarified, for the gift of one another's openness and sensitivity. Conclude with the following:

Leader   Let us pray:

All   Hail Mary, full of grace, the Lord is with thee!
         Blessed art thou among women,
         and blessed is the fruit of thy womb, Jesus.
         Holy Mary, mother of God, pray for us sinners,
         now and at the hour of our death. Amen

Leader   Come, Lord Jesus!

All   Come, Lord Jesus!

Christmas Season

Feast of the Holy Family

Family Life

Invitation to Pray

Pause for a few moments of silence and enter more deeply into the presence of God.

> *Song:* "Once in Royal David's City,"
> Cecil Francis Alexander
> Public Domain

> *Proclaim the gospel:* Luke 2:22-40
> The Child Grew and Became
> Strong, Filled with Wisdom

Take a few minutes to savour a word, a phrase, a question, or a feeling that rises up in you. Reflect on this quietly or share it aloud. (The other Scripture readings of the day are Genesis 15:1-6; 21:1-3 and Hebrews 11:8, 11-12, 17-19.)

Invitation to Reflect on the Gospel

The public perception of family life haschanged over the last 40 years. Now as never before families include single mothers and fathers with children, multi-generational families living together, grandparents raising grandchildren, couples with adopted children, couples with no children, step-parents and step-children, as well as married mothers and fathers with children. Families may be separated by divorce, death, temporary job assignments, college, prison, economic hardship, or immigration policies. Whatever their situation, each Christian family is called to be "a communion of persons, a sign and image of the communion of the Father and the Son in the Holy

27

Spirit" (*Catechism of the Catholic Church, 2205*). Each has its share of blessings and each has its piercing swords, as Simeon forewarned Mary in today's gospel. Each is a "community in which, from childhood, one can learn moral values, begin to honour God, and make good use of freedom…. The family should live in such a way that its members learn to care and take responsibility for the young, the old, the sick, the disabled, and the poor" (*Catechism, 2207-2208*). The mission of the family is the mission of the Church, and thus the family is often referred to as the domestic Church.

Among the challenges and graces of family life, few are more "interesting" than children's teenage years. The teenager's growing independence and self-definition can be emotionally turbulent, not only for the teenager, but also for parents and siblings. One father echoed the sentiments of many parents of teenagers in saying, "Instead of feeling like a sure role model and guide, I am more often a perplexed and confused parent, reeling from the hard knocks of life and the strong pull of the secular culture that threatens to engulf us…. I want so badly for my children to be moral and decent people; and Catholic, God willing." His advice to fellow parents of teenagers included the following: "Don't preach Catholicism, live it…. Put Catholic heroes before them…. Be forgiving of them and yourself…. Catholicism is the best path to God you've found…. Instill a sense of service…. Look for moments of grace, and you will see them."

Invitation to Group Sharing

1. What are some of the blessings and challenges that families currently experience in my neighbourhood, my parish, my town?

2. How did I come to know God and live out my faith from my family? How can I pass on this faith to my children, grandchildren, nieces/nephews?

3. How do my husband/wife and I express our faith in our marriage relationship? What can we do to enhance this aspect of our marriage?

4. How "family friendly" are the programmes and activities in our parish? What can we do to encourage such programmes?

Invitation to Act

Determine a specific action (individual or group) that flows from your sharing. This should be your primary consideration. When choosing an individual action, determine what you will do and share it with the group. When choosing a group action, determine who will take responsibility for different aspects of the action. The following are secondary suggestions:

1. Some religious groups ask families to establish "family night at home," – an evening each week when all members of the family are home and join together in family activities. Discuss this idea with your priest, your child's headteacher, and/or the parish cathechist, and suggest that it be encouraged among families in the parish.

2. Plan a parish family dinner event on the Feast of the Holy Family, and make sure that non-traditional families know they're welcome. Alternatively, begin a new family tradition by having a festive Holy Family feast day meal at home. Invite relatives that you may not have seen on Christmas Day, or another family or two, to join you.

3. Do a favour for a struggling family you know: offer to assist a single parent with childcare tasks so the parent can go grocery shopping, make dinner for a family in

which the parents are working multiple jobs or caring for aging or grandparents in care homes.

4. Ask your teenage children, grandchildren, nieces and/or nephews to volunteer with you at the local soup kitchen or in some other form of reaching out to others.

Invitation to Closing Prayer

Give thanks to God (aloud or silently) for insights gained, for desires awakened, for directions clarified, for the gift of one another's openness and sensitivity. Conclude with the following:

Side 1	God of our ancestors, you entrusted your Son to the care of Mary and Joseph.
Side 2	We praise you for the example of the Holy Family of Nazareth.
Side 1	You have made the family a privileged community of love and service.
Side 2	Guide our families in faith, hope, and charity.
Side 1	You have made us your sons and daughters in baptism.
Side 2	Bring us at life's end to the joy and peace of your eternal home.
Side 1	Glory be to the Father, and to the Son, and to the Holy Spirit,

Side 2	As it was in the beginning, is now, and will be forever. Amen
Side 1	The Word became flesh, alleluia!
Side 2	And dwelt among us, alleluia!

Mary, Mother of God

Searching for God in the World

Invitation to Pray

Pause for a few moments of silence and enter more deeply into the presence of God.

> ***Song:*** "As I kneel before you," Maria Parkinson,
> Kevin Mayhew Ltd

> ***Proclaim the gospel:*** Luke 2:16-21
> They Found Mary and Joseph and
> the Infant

Take a few minutes to savour a word, a phrase, a question, or a feeling that rises up in you. Reflect on this quietly or share it aloud. (The other Scripture readings of the day are Numbers 6:22-27 and Galatians 4:4-7.)

Invitation to Reflect on the Gospel

This reading picks up where the gospel for the Christmas Mass of Midnight leaves off. The shepherds come in search of the sign the angel had announced to them: "You will find an infant wrapped in swaddling clothes and lying in a manger" (Luke 2:12). Like the magi in the gospel for the Epiphany, the shepherds are searching for the newborn King, the Saviour, the Messiah, the Lord. Like the magi, the shepherds are "patron saints" for anyone who has ever asked, "Where is God?" Sometimes that question comes from what Saint John of the Cross described as "the dark night of the soul" – individual situations and entire chapters in one's life when doubt, adversity, or alienation leave one searching for meaning, for hope, for

God. Sometimes it is just the natural desire of the Christian, in the words of St. Ignatius of Loyola, to "find God in all things."

There are many examples of people searching for God in our Christian communities. The catechumens are asked to reflect further on the readings and to discern God's presence and action in their lives. Teenagers challenge us to make known in our individual and community lives the God whom we praise in our worship. The sick look for God in their suffering, and the grieving look for God in the death of a loved one. Spouses look for God in their marriage relationship, and children look for God in their families. Single people seek God in the serenity that comes from being alone, but not lonely. We are all, in some way, seekers, and the journey of seeking God has its ups and its downs, its highs and its lows. Baptism does not deliver us from this journey, nor does it guarantee that we will never harbour doubts or questions about God's presence. It does, however, incorporate us into a community that supports our search with its prayers and its faith. It also assures us that the God whom we seek promises to be with us in our searching.

Invitation to Group Sharing

1. How and where are people searching for spiritual meaning and for God today? What are the indications of this?

2. How do I seek God in my life? Am I able to "find God in all things"?

3. What have I learned about searching for God that I want to keep in mind during the times God does not seem very present to me?

4. Do I dismiss people's doubts and questions about faith or see them as expressions of the search to find and

know God? How do our community and our parish support people's search for God? How can we do this more explicitly?

Invitation to Act

Determine a specific action (individual or group) that flows from your sharing. This should be your primary consideration. When choosing an individual action, determine what you will do and share it with the group. When choosing a group action, determine who will take responsibility for different aspects of the action. The following are secondary suggestions:

1. Think of the people who have been helpful in your search for God and in the development of your faith. Thank them, and thank God for them.

2. Find out about opportunities for spiritual development in your area that complement what is offered in the parish, for example, retreat centres, spiritual directors, workshops, days of reflection. Develop a list of these resources that could be shared with members of the parish.

3. Investigate the possibility of a parish retreat. As a stimulus to group discussion about our search for God, invite a diverse group of parishioners to speak briefly about how and where they have found God. Some parishes have had success with family-oriented retreats that incorporate activities for various ages as well as opportunities for the whole group to come together.

Invitation to Closing Prayer

Give thanks to God (aloud or silently) for insights gained, for desires awakened, for directions clarified, for the gift of one another's openness and sensitivity. Conclude with the following:

Leader As we go forth to seek and serve God
in our lives,
let us pray together.

All May the Lord bless us and keep us!
May the Lord let his face shine upon us,
and be gracious to us!
May the Lord look upon us kindly
and give us peace!

All Amen

Leader The Word became flesh, alleluia!

All And dwelt among us, alleluia!

Second Sunday after Christmas

Jesus as Human and Divine

Invitation to Pray

Pause for a few moments of silence and enter more deeply into the presence of God.

> *Song:* "Jesus the Word has Lived Among Us," Keith D. Pearson, Joint Board of Christian Education of Australia & New Zealand
>
> *Proclaim the gospel:* John 1:1-18
> The Word Became Flesh and Made His Dwelling among Us

Take a few minutes to savour a word, a phrase, a question, or a feeling that rises up in you. Reflect on this quietly or share it aloud. (The other Scripture readings of the day are Sirach 24:1-2, 8-12 and Ephesians 1:3-6, 15-18.)

Invitation to Reflect on the Gospel

In those places where the celebration of the Epiphany has been transferred to a Sunday, the Second Sunday after Christmas is never celebrated. Fortunately, this passage from the beginning of John's Gospel also appears in the Mass for Christmas Day and in the weekday Mass for December 31. These eighteen verses are poetry, so be patient with yourself if their meaning is not immediately clear! John poetically explains that God revealed himself throughout history through the Scriptures and, ultimately, by taking on human flesh in Jesus. God's Word and God's light took flesh in Jesus who was human while remaining divine. We call this 'the Incarnation.'

Although it may sound like a remote theological concept, the Incarnation pervades Catholic beliefs and practices. When the nineteenth century Jesuit poet Gerard Manley Hopkins wrote, "The world is charged with the grandeur of God," he was tapping into an essentially Catholic attitude that sees God revealed in the 'stuff' of creation. God, who so embraced matter that he took on human flesh, continues to make himself known through the sacraments, especially the Eucharist, and in the created world. God, who once walked among us in human form, remains in our midst in bread and wine blessed and shared, in feet tenderly washed, in light kindled in darkness, in the love of a husband and wife, in water that washes and oil that seals. He is present in biblical words proclaimed and heard, in handshakes extended in peace, in vested ministers, and in the diverse men and women who gather in God's name for worship. We Catholics give pride of place to sacraments and sacramentals because, as Pope Leo the Great said in the fifth century, "what was visible in the Lord has passed over into the sacraments."

This gospel acknowledges that "no one has ever seen God" (John 1:18), yet this God came among us in the Incarnation, remains among us in the sacraments, dwells among us in the beauty of creation, and lives within us through the Holy Spirit. That's enough to make angels sing!

Invitation to Group Sharing

1. Why is the Incarnation so central to the Catholic faith? What does it mean to say that Jesus was both human and divine?

2. What does it mean to my faith that God took on human form and became "one of us"?

3. How are God's Word and God's light revealed in our world today? How are they revealed in my family, in our parish, and in the local community? In what ways can I reveal God's Word and God's light in my life this week?

Invitation to Act

Determine a specific action (individual or group) that flows from your sharing. This should be your primary consideration. When choosing an individual action, determine what you will do and share it with the group. When choosing a group action, determine who will take responsibility for different aspects of the action. The following are secondary suggestions:

1. The *Dogmatic Constitution on Divine Revelation* (*Dei Verbum*) is one of the shortest documents issued by the Second Vatican Council. Get a copy and read it. (Check your local Catholic bookshop for a collection of the Vatican II documents, or order it online from a service such as www.amazon.com.)

2. The "Introduction" to the *Lectionary for Mass* reminds us that "Christ is present in his Word" (Preamble, Chapter I.2.a.4) and that "God speaks to his people" (First Part, Chapter II.1.a.12) in the readings proclaimed at Mass. If you are a lector or reader in your parish, prepare your readings with this in mind. Treat the *Lectionary* with respect, and proclaim the reading with enthusiasm and understanding.

3. Reflect on your use of the resources of God's creation, and make efforts to protect and conserve them. Don't let water run unnecessarily. Use public transport when possible. Recycle. Turn the lights off when a room is empty.

Invitation to Closing Prayer

Give thanks to God (aloud or silently) for insights gained, for desires awakened, for directions clarified, for the gift of one another's openness and sensitivity. Conclude with the following:

Leader God of all creation,
your Word chose to dwell among us,
your true light came into our world.
Awaken us to your revelation in the Scriptures,
to Christ's presence in the sacraments,
and to the Spirit's pervading work in our world.
We ask this through Christ our Lord.

All Amen

Leader The Word became flesh, alleluia!

All And dwelt among us, alleluia!

The Epiphany of the Lord

God Manifests Himself to the World

Invitation to Pray

Pause for a few moments of silence and enter more deeply into the presence of God.

> *Song:* "As With Gladness,"
> William Chatterton Dix

> *Proclaim the gospel:* Matthew 2:1-12
> We Saw His Star at Its Rising and
> Have Come to Do Him Homage

Take a few minutes to savour a word, a phrase, a question, or a feeling that rises up in you. Reflect on this quietly or share it aloud. (The other Scripture readings of the day are Isaiah 60:1-6 and Ephesians 3:2-3a, 5-6.)

Invitation to Reflect on the Gospel

Have you ever found yourself in one of those situations where you said to God, "Please give me a sign"? Whether it's trying to make a difficult decision in the face of several options or trying to find God in the chaos of daily life, it's not unusual to want God to provide some kind of sign. From what we hear in today's gospel, people have been looking for such signs for a long time. In their search for the newborn King, the magi followed a star that brought them to the palace of King Herod and eventually to the manger where "they saw the child with Mary his mother" (Matthew 2:11).

Throughout the Christmas season, the Scriptures speak of how God has revealed himself to us. The unique point in today's gospel is that God chose to reveal himself not only to the beloved Jewish people, but also to the Gentiles, represented by the Magi. God manifests himself as God of the whole world, not just of a particular people. The star and the visit of the Magi to the Child Jesus were signs of this. What are the signs of this today? What are the signs in our world that God is for everyone, loves everyone, wants everyone to help promote or live the Kingdom of God on earth? Part of the answer involves a look in the mirror.

Collectively as the Body of Christ and individually as baptised Christians, we are called to be such signs; we are called to be stars that lead people to God. We call this 'evangelisation': bearing the Good News to a world that seeks meaning in life. In the words of Pope Paul VI, it is "bringing the Good News into all the strata of humanity, and through its influence transforming humanity from within and making it new" (*On Evangelisation in the Modern World,* 18). The primary way this happens is by the witness of our lives. This hope is well-expressed in the solemn blessing for the Epiphany Mass, taken from *The Roman Missal*:
"Because you are followers of Christ,
who appeared on this day as a light shining in darkness,
may he make you a light to all your sisters and brothers."

Invitation to Group Sharing

1. What are the signs in today's world that God embraces all of humanity? How does God manifest himself in our world today?

2. What are the signs I encounter that make me aware of God's presence in my life?

3. In what ways do I serve as a sign that leads others to God? In what ways do I not lead others to God? How can I be a better sign for others?

Invitation to Act

Determine a specific action (individual or group) that flows from your sharing. This should be your primary consideration. When choosing an individual action, determine what you will do and share it with the group. When choosing a group action, determine who will take responsibility for different aspects of the action. The following are secondary suggestions:

1. Get a copy of *On Evangelisation in the Modern World*, Pope Paul VI's apostolic exhortation to all Catholics to proclaim the gospel. Read and discuss it in your group.

2. Think about the people in your local community who may be alienated from the Church. Consider ways to reach out to them.

3. Talk to the priest or parish pastoral council about starting a new parishioner welcome programme. In some parishes, a parishioner visits the home of newly registered parishioners to welcome them, bringing a basket of baked goods and information about the parish. Host a reception after Mass once or twice a year for new parishioners, and ask other parishioners to attend and welcome the newcomers.

4. It is a custom in some places to bless homes at the time of the Epiphany. Plan an Epiphany meal with family or friends, and celebrate a blessing of your home.

Invitation to Closing Prayer

Give thanks to God (aloud or silently) for insights gained, for desires awakened, for directions clarified, for the gift of one another's openness and sensitivity. Conclude with the following:

Leader   Lord of all nations, Father of us all,
throughout the ages you have given us signs
of your presence and action in the world.
May your light shine
through our words and our deeds
that those whom we meet
may find their way to you.
We ask this through Christ our Lord,
who lives and reigns with you,
Father, and the Holy Spirit,
one God forever and ever.

All   Amen

Leader   The Word became flesh, alleluia!

All   And dwelt among us, alleluia!

The Baptism of the Lord

Mission of Service

Invitation to Pray

Pause for a few moments of silence and enter more deeply into the presence of God.

> ***Song:*** "When Jesus Comes to be Baptised,"
> The Benedictines of Stanbrook

> ***Proclaim the gospel:*** Mark 1:7-11
> You Are My Beloved Son;
> With You I Am Well Pleased

Take a few minutes to savour a word, a phrase, a question, or a feeling that rises up in you. Reflect on this quietly or share it aloud. (The other Scripture readings of the day are Isaiah 55:1-11 and 1 John 5:1-9.)

Invitation to Reflect on the Gospel

This reading picks up where the gospel on the Second Sunday of Advent left off, with John the Baptist pointing away from himself and towards "one mightier than I…[who] will baptise you with the Holy Spirit" (Mark 1:7, 8). Jesus is then baptised by John, the Spirit descends upon him, and a heavenly voice declares him "my beloved Son" (Mark 1:11). Like the other feasts of the Christmas season, the Baptism of the Lord is another chapter in the unfolding manifestation of Jesus as the Messiah sent by God. The particular focus of this final day of the Christmas season is the inauguration of Jesus' public mission. Throughout the rest of the liturgical year, we see that mission unfold in Jesus' words and deeds, ultimately leading to his death and Resurrection.

As with the proclamation of Scripture in any liturgy, the point of this reading is not just to learn something about the life of Jesus, but to shape our own lives ever more closely to the life that Jesus modelled for us. When we say "Praise to you, Lord Jesus Christ" at the end of this gospel, we not only acclaim Christ, whose mission was divinely announced at his baptism, but we also affirm that mission as our own. In the waters of our baptism, we were joined to the mission Christ publicly began as he emerged from the Jordan River. In each Eucharist, we renew our commitment to that mission. As Pope John Paul II said at the Fifteenth World Youth Day, "To celebrate the Eucharist, 'to eat his flesh and drink his blood,' means to accept the wisdom of the Cross and the path of service. It means that we signal our willingness to sacrifice ourselves for others, as Christ has done" (*Closing Homily* 5, 20th August 2000). Two years earlier, he made a similar connection between our worship and service when he said, "The Roman Rite has always been a form of worship that looks to mission" (*Ad Limina* Address of the Pope to the Bishops of the Church in Washington, Oregon, Montana, Idaho and Alaska, October 9, 1998).

As baptism was the inauguration of Jesus' public mission, so baptism is but the beginning of each Christian's mission to serve as Jesus served. This feast offers each of us an opportunity to reflect on how we are living out that mission in our daily lives.

Invitation to Group Sharing

1. What does it mean to live out the mission of Christ in my life?

2. In what ways am I using my God-given talents to promote Christ's mission?

3. Who are some people who are living out Christ's mission in our world and in our local community, and how do their lives of witness speak to me?

4. How involved is our parish in service to those outside of our community? What might be done to strengthen this essential part of our parish life and mission?

Invitation to Act

Determine a specific action (individual or group) that flows from your sharing. This should be your primary consideration. When choosing an individual action, determine what you will do and share it with the group. When choosing a group action, determine who will take responsibility for different aspects of the action. The following are secondary suggestions:

1. Though they may not be as active in some aspects of Church life, many Catholic young adults are drawn to opportunities for service. Talk to the priest or parish pastoral council about offering such opportunities in your parish. For ideas, read the *At Your Word, Lord* Season V Action Pack.

2. Learn more about the celebration of baptism and its connection to mission. See the videos *Baptism* by Catholic Faith Exploration (www.faithcafe.org/baptism.htm) *This Is the Night: A Parish Welcomes New Members*, which focuses on adult initiation (available at good Catholic bookshops).

3. In the *Rite of Christian Initiation of Adults (RCIA)*, sponsors help catechumens to shape their lives according to the model and mission of Christ. It's an opportunity for spiritual growth for the sponsor as much as it is for the catechumen. Consider volunteering to serve as a sponsor for a catechumen in your parish's *RCIA*. See the book *Foundations in Faith: Handbook for Sponsors* edited by Karen Griffiths (available through good Catholic bookshops).

4. Offer to assist in your parish's infant baptism ministry.

Invitation to Closing Prayer

Give thanks to God (aloud or silently) for insights gained, for desires awakened, for directions clarified, for the gift of one another's openness and sensitivity. Conclude with the following:

Side 1   God of love, you revealed Jesus
as your beloved Son in the Jordan River.

Side 2   We praise you for the gift of Christ,
our salvation and our peace.

Side 1   You anointed Jesus for the service of
the world.

Side 2   Strengthen the Church's witness
to this mission in our world today.

Side 1   You brought us to new life and made us
members of Christ's Body in baptism.

Side 2   May the gift of your Holy Spirit keep us
ready to meet the demands of our baptism.

Side 1   Glory be to the Father, and to the Son,
and to the Holy Spirit,

Side 2   As it was in the beginning, is now
and will be forever. Amen

Side 1   The Word became flesh, alleluia!

Side 2   And dwelt among us, alleluia!

Lenten Season

First Sunday of Lent

Renewal

Invitation to Pray

Pause for a few moments of silence and enter more deeply into the presence of God.

> *Song:* "Led by the Spirit of our God,"
> Bob Hurd, OCP

> *Proclaim the gospel:* Mark 1:12-15
> The Temptation of Jesus

Take a few minutes to savour a word, a phrase, a question, or a feeling that rises up in you. Reflect on this quietly or share it aloud. (The other Scripture readings of the day are Genesis 9:8-15 and 1 Peter 3:18-22.)

Invitation to Reflect on the Gospel

As Lent begins, and the catechumens enter into their final phase of preparation for baptism, the whole Church begins a period of spiritual renewal leading to Easter. Lent is a time of retreat. We journey inwardly to the desert places of solitude and silence to rediscover God's unique and abiding love for us. This love strengthens us for our mission in the world.

Before the beginning of his public ministry, Jesus is driven into the wilderness by the Spirit to fast and pray. He is about to undertake his mission and must prepare by putting all other things aside. His sojourn in the desert is a time of serious, focused prayer. Like Jesus, we, too, are impelled by the Spirit to get down to basics during Lent. If we are to renew the covenant of baptism, which empowers us to love and serve others, we must put aside whatever is not essential in our lives and take the risk of entrusting ourselves completely to God in prayer. The wild beasts of our fears and sinfulness may cause us anxiety as we stand before God in prayer, but the angels of hope and trust come there to minister to us. We must be attentive to the Spirit's promptings to put aside the nonessentials and make a specific commitment to prayer this Lent.

Unlike Matthew and Luke, Mark says nothing about the content of the temptations that Jesus faced in the desert. Nor does Mark say that the temptations ended, but only that Satan left Jesus to await another opportunity. In fact, throughout Mark's Gospel, Satan continues to test Jesus, all the way to the cross. Yet Jesus perseveres. His time in the wilderness strengthens him for all that lies ahead. This gives us hope, for the Christian, too, must wrestle with demons not only once, but repeatedly during life's journey.

Invitation to Group Sharing

1. What are some examples of how secondary things and nonessentials take on greater importance than they should in my life? In my parish? In my neighbourhood?

2. How ready am I to make a fresh start in my practice of prayer this Lent? What attracts me about the prospect of spending more time with God in prayer? What makes me uneasy or doubtful? What specific prayer commitment can I make for Lent?

3. What are some personal disciplines I can undertake this Lent to rededicate myself to an honest and vital relationship with the God who loves me?

Invitation to Act

Determine a specific action (individual or group) that flows from your sharing. This should be your primary consideration. When choosing an individual action, determine what you will do and share it with the group. When choosing a group action, determine who will take responsibility for different aspects of the action. The following are secondary suggestions:

1. Make a list of spiritual priorities for this season, and keep it somewhere you will see it often. Ask yourself at the end of each day: "Have my actions reflected these priorities?"

2. Ask your priest and the chairperson of the parish council to incorporate faith sharing in all parish meetings for the remainder of the Lenten season.

3. Fast from asking God for things in prayer. Focus instead on thanksgiving, praise, and contemplation for a set period of time each day.

4. Choose a quiet need in your neighbourhood that normally gets lost in the shuffle of noisier problems and issues, and make a concrete contribution to taking care of that need.

Invitation to Closing Prayer

Give thanks to God (aloud or silently) for insights gained, for desires awakened, for directions clarified, for the gift of one another's openness and sensitivity. Conclude with the following:

Side 1   God of the covenant, just as your Spirit
sent Jesus into the wilderness, so you have
sent us, your people, into the desert of Lent.

Side 2   Doubtful and fearful we come,
confused by the whirlwind pace of our lives,
and the clamour of lesser voices.

Side 1   Yet we long for the simplicity and strength
of a life centered in you, O God,
source of our joy and our peace.

Side 2   Help us to enter the desert of Lent,
and, leaving all else aside,
let us rest in you alone.

All   Amen

Second Sunday of Lent

Religious Experience

Invitation to Pray

Pause for a few moments of silence and enter more deeply into the presence of God.

> *Song:* "How Good, Lord, to be Here,"
> J Armitage Robinson

> *Proclaim the gospel:* Mark 9:2-10
> Transfiguration of Jesus

Take a few minutes to savour a word, a phrase, a question, or a feeling that rises up in you. Reflect on this quietly or share it aloud. (The other Scripture readings of the day are Genesis 22:1-2, 9a, 10-13, 15-18 and Romans 8:31b-34.)

Invitation to Reflect on the Gospel

Most of us probably think we would welcome the opportunity to see Jesus in his glory. But when the disciples, Peter, James, and John, witnessed the transfiguration, they were both attracted by what they saw and overwhelmed by fear. In their journey with Jesus thus far, they had learned to revere him as master and teacher, and they had walked the dusty roads of Palestine with him as companion and friend. Here, on the high mountain, however, they catch a glimpse of his divinity, and it is an awesome sight indeed. Not only do they see Jesus with light streaming forth from his garments, they also see him in conversation with the greatest figures of the Jewish religious tradition: Moses (giver of the Law) and Elijah (foremost among the prophets). One wonders what they were talking about. By the time the voice from heaven tells the disciples to "listen to him" (Mark 9:7) however, there is no more conversation to overhear. The vision is over, and Jesus alone is left with them to speak about his coming suffering and death. The dazzling clothing and the breath-taking appearance of saintly figures dissolve into talk of the dark and hard future that presses on Jesus – probably the last thing the disciples expected to hear. They leave the mountain puzzled, even as present day disciples also feel consternation at the twists and turns of their calling in this world. Yet they are changed by what they have seen, even if they do not perfectly understand it. They have been called to a deeper attention to Jesus' words, actions, and presence in their midst.

At times believers have 'mountaintop experiences' of faith, and catch glimpses of the glorious truth of God in Christ. An experience of this kind can cause a permanent change. The test of its effectiveness, however, is not in the powerful feelings the experience evoked, but in the capacity to listen to Jesus' paradoxical message of self-sacrifice after the experience is over.

Invitation to Group Sharing

1. What have my own 'mountaintop' experiences of faith been like? What effects have these experiences had on me?

2. Why is it sometimes difficult for us to 'listen to' Jesus, either individually or as a parish community? What are some examples of times when we have listened well?

3. Does the divinity of Jesus attract me or overwhelm me? If I were to imagine Jesus in conversation with two great figures from the Christian tradition, who would they be? What would they be saying?

4. Sunday worship should capture some of the awesome majesty of God as well as God's fascinating nearness. What are some moments of awe and fascination in the liturgy, as we experience it?

Invitation to Act

Determine a specific action (individual or group) that flows from your sharing. This should be your primary consideration. When choosing an individual action, determine what you will do and share it with the group. When choosing a group action, determine who will take responsibility for different aspects of the action. The following are secondary suggestions:

1. Spend some time in silent meditation each day this week. Afterward, reflect on or jot down a thought or feeling that rose up within you during this meditation time. At the end of the week, share your experience with at least one other person in your group.

2. Take part with others in an activity of direct service to people who are suffering or in need, and notice God's gifts in the people who 'carry a cross' today.

3. Seek out a special place of beauty to visit this week. Let the serenity and grandeur or the sheer simplicity of this beautiful place heal your soul.

4. Write a 'thank you' letter to someone who has helped you to be a stronger, more courageous Christian, and share the results with others in your group.

Invitation to Closing Prayer

Give thanks to God (aloud or silently) for insights gained, for desires awakened, for directions clarified, for the gift of one another's openness and sensitivity. Conclude with the following:

> Psalm 121
>
> I raise my eyes toward the mountains.
> > From where will my help come?
> My help comes from the LORD,
> > the maker of heaven and earth.
>
> God will not allow your foot to slip;
> > your guardian does not sleep.
> Truly, the guardian of Israel
> > never slumbers or sleeps.
> The LORD is your guardian;
> > the LORD is your shade
> > at your right hand.
> By day the sun cannot harm you,
> > nor the moon by night.
> The LORD will guard you from all evil,
> > will always guard your life.
> The LORD will guard your coming and going
> > both now and forever.

Third Sunday of Lent

Prophetic Zeal of Jesus

Invitation to Pray

Pause for a few moments of silence and enter more deeply into the presence of God.

> ***Song:*** "Awake, Awake, Fling off the Night,' J.R. Peacey, Mrs Mildrew Peacey

> ***Proclaim the gospel:*** John 2:13-25
> The New Temple

Take a few minutes to savour a word, a phrase, a question, or a feeling that rises up in you. Reflect on this quietly or share it aloud. (The other Scripture readings of the day are Exodus 20:1-17 and 1 Corinthians 1:22-25.)

Invitation to Reflect on the Gospel

For pious Jews of his day, and indeed for Jesus himself, the Temple in Jerusalem was a sacred place. It was the special dwelling of God in the midst of a holy city. The Temple was a centre of pilgrimage for Jews from all over the known world, and a place where ritual sacrifices and prayers were offered. Scripture scholars have observed that the presence of money changers and merchants selling animals was probably quite common in the outer courtyard of the Temple, due to the phenomenon of pilgrims. Anyone coming to the Temple from a long distance to make a ritual sacrifice would naturally find it easier to buy an animal on the spot rather than bring one from home, and in order to make this purchase would need to change money. Moreover, men paid the Temple tax in coins without an image so exchange services were needed.

We should not imagine, therefore, that the scene that so upsets Jesus is a spectacle of wild debauchery or obvious corruption. Nor should we conclude that he was opposed to Temple sacrifices or other cultic practices of the Judaism of his day. His own mother offered sacrifice at the time of his birth. What causes Jesus to explode in indignation is, outwardly at least, 'business as usual' – practices which the average person would not have even noticed. Turning over tables, he exposed what was in human hearts. Beneath the expedients of the day, there was a crumbling of the original impulse of worship. Faith and devotion to God had collapsed into compromises of convenience and convention. His bold gestures proclaim: Conventional religion is not enough. Faith is not a matter of convenience. We must be in love with God. We must be passionate about worship and prayer. We must live the covenant with God fully. Jesus himself shows us how to be passionate. He speaks, thinks, and acts boldly. The zeal of Jesus leads him to the cross ("destroy this temple") and Resurrection ("I will raise it up") (John 2:19). It is the source of new and passionate faith, which rebuilds the temple of humanity's relationship with God.

Invitation to Group Sharing

1. Have I experienced a time of lukewarm faith? What re-awakened my zeal for God?

2. What can we do to awaken ourselves from 'business as usual' to a more lively faith?

3. What would be the 'signs' of such a change of heart in my life?

Invitation to Act

Determine a specific action (individual or group) that flows from your sharing. This should be your primary consideration. When choosing an individual action, determine what you will do and share it with the group. When choosing a group action, determine who will take responsibility for different aspects of the action. The following are secondary suggestions:

1. As a family, spend some time at the beginning of your meal together to share what you most cherish about God or your faith. You might want to mention how you saw God active in your life that day.

2. Reach out to someone you know whose faith is 'lukewarm', in a way that affirms that person's goodness. Invite him or her to come with you to a parish activity.

3. Imagine in prayer that your own life is a temple in which God dwells. Imagine that Jesus visits that temple. What will he see that needs to be "driven out" so God can fill the whole of your life? Invite him to help you change.

4. Take an inventory of the physical areas that parishioners see when they come to Mass, asking, "What is conducive to worship?" Talk with the parish team about your suggestions for improvement.

Invitation to Closing Prayer

Give thanks to God (aloud or silently) for insights gained, for desires awakened, for directions clarified, for the gift of one another's openness and sensitivity. Conclude with the following:

> Jesus, our Saviour and Lord,
> teach us to welcome you as you are.
>
> Do not spare us
> the flame of your indignation at lukewarm faith,
> the fire of your anger at compromises with injustice,
> the blaze of your purifying love.
>
> Awaken in us a passionate love for God and neighbour.
> Inspire us to boldness as we encounter our own trials of faith.
> Empower us with zeal for your holy Church,
> truly the place where the Spirit dwells.
>
> Thank you for this community, which you have given us.
> Strengthen us as we strengthen one another
> in faith, hope, and love. Amen

Fourth Sunday of Lent

God's Love for the World

Invitation to Pray

Pause for a few moments of silence and enter more deeply into the presence of God.

> *Song:* "Lift High the Cross," Sydney H. Nicholson

> *Proclaim the gospel:* John 3:14-21
> Jesus Lifted Up in Death and
> Exaltation

Take a few minutes to savour a word, a phrase, a question, or a feeling that rises up in you. Reflect on this quietly or share it aloud. (The other Scripture readings of the day are 2 Chronicles 36:14-16, 19-23 and Ephesians 2:4-10.)

Invitation to Reflect on the Gospel

The Old Testament recounts many episodes that took place during the forty years Israel spent in the desert, after their Exodus from Egypt and before they entered the promised land. One such episode is mentioned in today's gospel reading: The chosen people were attacked by poisonous serpents, as punishment for their unfaithfulness (see Numbers 21:4-9), and were only saved from death by God's intervention through Moses. God tells Moses to lift up a bronze image of a serpent, and everyone who looks at the serpent is healed.

Jesus uses the image of Moses and the bronze serpent to foreshadow his own death, when he will be "lifted up" (John 3:14) on the crossbeam of wood. The crucifixion is presented as the means of healing for all who see it in faith. The Evangelist is careful to present the universal scope of God's saving love. Salvation is not intended for only a few. Eternal life and the healing of the wounds of sin are gifts offered to all people. They are offered through the Son of God, out of God's deep and abiding love. This passage should lay to rest any fears that God may be like a 'hanging judge' who shakes a finger at us from heaven and sends Jesus down to condemn us for our sins. Instead, God is so much in love with us that he hands over his Son to ransom all people from bondage to sin and death.

God's love in Christ is unconditional, but a free response is needed for the gift to be received. The chilling reality is that people can indeed decide to look away from the truth of God's love and choose evil over good. Thus we are left to consider what choice we will make. Do we remain in the gloom of night, or will we choose to come into the light of goodness, truth, and faith?

Nicodemus is the man who came to Jesus at night, asking if a person can be born again (John 3:4). He is a seeker who desires salvation, and this further dialogue of Jesus with Nicodemus is a way of speaking about the new life of faith and baptism. In the Lenten season, as candidates prepare for baptism, the faithful also revisit fundamental questions as we move together toward the glory of Easter.

Invitation to Group Sharing

1. What stories of seekers, such as the catechumens at my parish, have touched me and made me more aware of faith as a gift that must be freely embraced?

2. What is my image of God? Do I have trouble believing that God loves all the peoples of the world, regardless of race, ethnicity, gender, religion, or way of life? In

what way do I have difficulty believing that God loves *me*, regardless of my past or present sinfulness?

3. How can I return to the font of baptism this Easter and recapture the truth of God's unconditional love for me?

4. How can I help others I meet to come into the light of faith, step-by-step each day?

Invitation to Act

Determine a specific action (individual or group) that flows from your sharing. This should be your primary consideration. When choosing an individual action, determine what you will do and share it with the group. When choosing a group action, determine who will take responsibility for different aspects of the action. The following are secondary suggestions:

1. Make a point of talking with one or more adults who are preparing for baptism at Easter. Ask them what has helped them along their journey of faith. Keep them in your prayers during this season, as 'fellow pilgrims.'

2. Revisit your own baptism by retrieving a photo, baptismal certificate, or memento of the event and sharing it with others in your group. Spend some time in prayer thanking God for the people who brought you to baptism and the Christian life.

3. Abstain from jokes and conversations that put down the family or neighbourhood scapegoat or other people because of race, gender, ethnicity, or religion. Think of ways to challenge or redirect situations that foster disrespectful attitudes.

4. Affirm a child or teenager for taking part in religious education and catechesis. Invite him or her to tell you about what he or she is learning and doing in the programme.

Invitation to Closing Prayer

Give thanks to God (aloud or silently) for insights gained, for desires awakened, for directions clarified, for the gift of one another's openness and sensitivity. Conclude with the following:

Place a crucifix in a place where all can see it, and take a few moments in silence to contemplate the love of God poured out in Jesus' sacrifice on the cross.

God, Father of infinite mercy,
you do not consider our faults and failings,
but reach out to us and to all people
with compassion and love.

Through the cross of your beloved Son,
help us to recognise your gift and your victory,
and to respond with faith.
We ask this through Christ our Lord. Amen

Fifth Sunday of Lent

Ministry as Sharing

Invitation to Pray

Pause for a few moments of silence and enter more deeply into the presence of God.

> *Song:* "Unless a Grain of Wheat,"
> Bernadette Farrell, OCP

> *Proclaim the gospel:* John 12:20-33
> The Father Will Honour Those
> Who Serve Me

Take a few minutes to savour a word, a phrase, a question, or a feeling that rises up in you. Reflect on this quietly or share it aloud. (The other Scripture readings of the day are Jeremiah 31:31-34 and Hebrews 5:7-9.)

Invitation to Reflect on the Gospel

This passage is the closest John's Gospel ever gets to a Garden of Gethsemane scene. John portrays Jesus as in control of all the events that are happening to him. Jesus is in complete harmony with all that the Father desires. The words and actions of Jesus are the perfect expression of the Father's wishes. They are so aligned with one another that to see Jesus is to be in touch with God.

In the gospel, Jesus' hour is the moment of his death, which is at the same time, the moment of his glorification. "And when I am lifted up from the earth, I will draw everyone to myself" (John 12:32). John's indication of how Jesus is to die also becomes his way of saying that in death, community and unity with God will be fully accomplished in and through Jesus. It is the moment of his death, as well as the moment of glorification and exaltation of God. God is totally praised and glorified in Jesus' action and love. The Father's response to Jesus' love and fidelity is the glorification and exaltation of Jesus through the Resurrection.

Jesus' ministry in our midst, his fidelity to the Father, and his service to others in love, even to the point of death, gives a model of what it means to be truly human. To be human is to glorify God in and through our ministry of service to all we encounter. That ministry involves the total sharing with all of the many gifts we have been given. That ministry may take the form, for example, of ministering to an aged parent or a disabled child. It may be a call to minister to a hurting colleague or a troubled teenager.

We are called to serve others. Jesus has provided the model for us to understand how to do this well. That model involves walking the path that Jesus walked. We know the path leads to the point of death, the 'hour' of the gospel. "Whoever serves me must follow me, and where I am, there also will my servant be" (John 12:26). But we also know that the hour that involves death to self is the only path to exaltation and glory. In so doing, we glorify God, and God, in return, glorifies us.

Service of others is not easy and often challenges our willingness and determination to share what we have been given. This is difficult for us, especially when we experience rejection, lack of response, or lack of appreciation from those we serve. Yet, "unless the grain of wheat falls to the ground and dies, it remains just a grain of wheat; but if it dies it produces much fruit" (John 12:24).

This is not an easy task. Even Jesus reacts, "I am troubled now" (John 12:27). The temptation to flee the "hour" is strong Yet Jesus knows that all he has been doing has led to this reality. How can he pull back now? He doesn't. With his help, neither will we. Like Jesus, service, at whatever price, is what we are all about. We do all we can, and we let God do the rest. Let us work on allowing our grain of wheat to fall to the ground and die so that it will produce much fruit.

Invitation to Group Sharing

1. When have I encountered difficulties in life, especially at times when I have consistently tried to be honest, loving, and of service to others? What feelings surfaced and what questions were generated in me because of the experience?

2. How have I handled the perennial temptation to deny, run away from, or refuse to face the many challenges that following Christ entails? What comfort do I draw from my reflections on this particular gospel passage?

3. How do I counter the constant social pressure that pushes us to acquire more and more in order to be happy and fulfilled? How do I share what I have with others?

4. Share how ministry, whatever it might be, calls one forth to care for and work with others, even at great cost or sacrifice. What makes me want to enter into this sort of sacrificing for others? How will I enter into this sacrifice more readily?

Invitation to Act

Determine a specific action (individual or group) that flows from your sharing. This should be your primary consideration. When choosing an individual action, determine what you will do and share it with the group. When choosing a group action, determine who will take responsibility for different aspects of the action. The following are secondary suggestions:

1. Seek out people who are known for their wisdom and understanding in dealing with life in a context of faith. Make these people your mentors and guides. When the journey gets tough, ask them to be companions with you. If you already have a mentor of the faith, send a note of thanks celebrating his or her presence in your life.

2. Interview those who are involved in challenging ministries, full of frustrations and setbacks. Determine what enables these ministers to persevere. Learn and grow from that knowledge when difficulties arise in your own life and ministry.

3. Take time to pray and discern what your gifts are and what the best way is to share those gifts with others.

4. Cultivate a sense of giving and letting go. Every six months, let go of clothes or possessions you have not used or will not use again. Continually determine if you really need all that you have and let go of what is not really essential. Use the following criteria: "Take what you need. No more and no less. Give the rest away."

Invitation to Closing Prayer

Give thanks to God (aloud or silently) for insights gained, for desires awakened, for directions clarified, for the gift of one another's openness and sensitivity. Conclude with the following:

> O strong and loving Jesus,
> You have taught us so many things
> by your life and ministry.
> You model so marvellously for us
> what a loving relationship
> with God the Father is all about.
> Help us to model ourselves on you.
> Send us the power of the Spirit
> to strengthen us when we falter
> or are tempted to back away from the demands of love.
> May our ministry truly be one of sharing
> all that we have with others.
> We ask this in your name, united in you,
> with the Father and the Spirit, now and always. Amen

Palm Sunday of the Lord's Passion

Passion of Jesus Christ

Invitation to Pray

Pause for a few moments of silence and enter more deeply into the presence of God.

> *Song:* "All Glory, Laud and Honour," St Theodulph of Orleans, tr. John Mason Neale

> *Proclaim the gospel:* Mark 14:1-15:47
> Truly This Was the Son of God

Take a few minutes to savour a word, a phrase, a question, or a feeling that rises up in you. Reflect on this quietly or share it aloud. (The other Scripture readings of the day are Isaiah 50:4-7 and Philippians 2:6-11.)

Invitation to Reflect on the Gospel

The passion, for Mark, is the final expression of the confrontation that Jesus has been having with the forces of evil since his struggles began in the desert at the very beginning of his ministry (Mark 1:12-13). Jesus' fidelity to his mission to overcome evil and defeat its every manifestation has generated a coming together of those very forces with the explicit mission to undo him. Yet Jesus continues to be faithful to what he knows to be his mission – the proclamation of the Good News that God's reign is here and that the evil one is defeated. In the meantime, Jesus must experience the full impact of his humanity, as well as experience the questioning that is at the heart of any believer.

In Mark's passion account, the forces of evil have mustered their strength against Jesus and seem about to defeat him. This situation overwhelms and appears to overcome Jesus. Yet, in fidelity to his mission, he continues to journey the path in hope and in trust. This hope and trust are truly tested in the passion. Mark presents Jesus as turning to Psalm 22 in his trial: "My God, my God, why have you forsaken me?" (Mark 15:34). Some may interpret these words as doubt and despair before the power of death. Yet Jesus enters into it with the fullness of hope and trust in his Father who has been with him throughout and who will continue to be with him even in this, the very depths of death. Jesus places his ultimate trust in God. And God is not blind to that hope and trust.

In the meantime, this sort of death activates awareness, insight, and hope from others whom one would least expect. The centurion, a Gentile and supposedly a non-believer, can proclaim with certainty that "Truly this man was the Son of God!" (Mark 15:39). Simon of Cyrene, the model disciple for Mark, is willing to carry the cross for Jesus. Mark presents us with a portrait of Jesus who is faithful to his mission and consistently trusts in God no matter what the cost.

Discipleship demands the same for all who take up the challenge to follow Jesus. We, too, must be willing to take up the cross and walk whatever path is demanded of us, for example, serious illness or the death of a loved one. We, too, must be willing to have trust and hope, even when despair seems to overwhelm. We, too, must be willing to believe even when we do not understand why something is happening or what good will ever come out of it. Can we trust God to be faithful, to be attentive to our cry, and to act on our behalf to accomplish nothing but good? This is what we mean by the Paschal Mystery. This is what we mean by the Resurrection. Do we really believe this is operative in our lives here and now? Jesus has walked the path before us. Dare we follow?

Invitation to Group Sharing

1. How does Mark's portrayal of Jesus model the way we are to deal with our own suffering? How does this model fit my image of God and how God relates to us in our suffering?

2. How do I understand Jesus' cry from the cross: "My God, my God, why have you forsaken me?" (Mark 15:34). Does it point to the entire Psalm 22 and express a deeper trust and hope in God? Or is it merely a cry of loneliness, despair, and abandonment? How does this relate to my image of Jesus?

3. Share how you have continued to take up whatever cross has been given to you in your life. What have I learned from my daily struggle to carry my cross with Jesus? Mention feelings and emotions that are part and parcel of this daily living.

4. What is my understanding of the term 'Paschal Mystery'? What significance does it have for my daily living? How should our lives be different as a result of this belief? What will I do differently as a result of this faith stance?

Invitation to Act

Determine a specific action (individual or group) that flows from your sharing. This should be your primary consideration. When choosing an individual action, determine what you will do and share it with the group. When choosing a group action, determine who will take responsibility for different aspects of the action. The following are secondary suggestions:

1. Pray the Stations of the Cross as a group. Allow your follow-up discussion to focus on God's presence and activity in the midst of suffering.

2. Call a person who is struggling with pain and suffering of any kind and offer to be a listening ear or to lend a helping hand. Get suggestions of people to contact from your parish pastoral care ministers.

3. Offer to volunteer at a hospice with those helping others to die with love and dignity. After this experience, reflect on its meaning for you.

4. Offer to take people to a service of the anointing of the sick. Be present with them and celebrate the sacrament with them, praying for God's touch and presence no matter what the results of the sickness may be.

Invitation to Closing Prayer

Give thanks to God (aloud or silently) for insights gained, for desires awakened, for directions clarified, for the gift of one another's openness and sensitivity. Conclude with the following:

Loving and faithful Jesus,

We thank you for the way you generously gave yourself - even to dying on a cross for us.

You have shown us what it means to be truly human, accepting all that human living entails, even death.

In plumbing the fullness of death, you continually trusted in your Father, relying on his love and fidelity.

Help us to develop that same trust in God,
to grow in the virtue of hope.

Be with us as we face the constant deaths of daily existence,
as well as when we plumb the fullness of our own death.

Be our constant companion and guide.
Lead us to continued life
united with the Father and the Spirit.

We ask this in continual trust and confidence,
now and forever. Amen

Easter Season

Easter Sunday

Presence and Absence of God

Invitation to Pray

Pause for a few moments of silence and enter more deeply into the presence of God.

> *Song:* "Jesus Christ is Risen Today," Lyra Davidica, Public Domain

> *Proclaim the gospel:* John 20:1-9
> The Empty Tomb Experience of Mary Magdalene and Two of the Disciples

Take a few minutes to savour a word, a phrase, a question, or a feeling that rises up in you. Reflect on this quietly or share it aloud. (The other Scripture readings of the day are Acts 10:34a, 37-43 and Colossians 3:1-4 or 1 Corinthians 5:6b-8.)

Invitation to Reflect on the Gospel

The various characters in today's gospel are models for us and for anyone searching in faith, trying to make sense and under-stand what they see or do not see. Faith is, like Mary Magdalene, seeking contact with God even though a situation might appear hopeless. When Mary gets to the tomb, she expected one thing and saw and experienced another. She did not understand and went back to the community of disciples to help her understand. This is an important step for Mary and for any who attempt to make sense of where the Lord is present and how we can be in touch with him.

The others in this passage also need to see for themselves where the Lord is present and how to get in touch with him. Peter and the "other" disciple whom Jesus loved both run to the tomb to see and to understand. When they get there, Peter sees but it appears that he does not understand and cannot make sense of what he is seeing. The other disciple whom Jesus loved sees and believes. The contrast between the two is striking. Yet, what is the difference in their reaction when they both witness the same thing?

Seeing is a constant metaphor in the gospels for coming to faith. But merely seeing with one's eyes is not enough. One has to be open to the possibility of seeing things that are utterly unexpected and that make very little or no sense, especially when seen with the same old lenses. The seeing has to be open to the presence of God in new and totally unexpected ways. People have found God in the birth of a child, in a letter received from a prisoner on death row, in soup kitchens and while waiting in the bus queue, in the beauty of a sunset, or in a flowering meadow.

The old lenses, which see the old patterns of thinking, doing, and making sense of things, no longer help. The Lord will not be found there. Rather, new perspectives, new viewpoints, new places, and new times are demanded. There the Lord will be found. In places where we least expect, the Lord makes himself manifest and present.

How open are we to trying on new lenses, to seeing in ways we have not experienced before? This is the demand of faith, the stance that will open us to possibilities not even yet imagined. This is what will open us to experiencing Jesus resurrected, Jesus intimately with us, Jesus present in ways we never expected.

Invitation to Group Sharing

1. To what people or to what places might I look where I previously did not expect to find Jesus?

2. How does my faith help me make sense of things that go counter to what I am expecting or would like to happen?

3. To whom do I go for help to try to make sense of the unexpected in life, especially the surprises that challenge my core beliefs and values?

4. How do we, as a community of faith, help one another walk through the difficult, unexpected times in our lives? How do we help one another expand our understanding of who God is and how God operates in our midst?

Invitation to Act

Determine a specific action (individual or group) that flows from your sharing. This should be your primary consideration. When choosing an individual action, determine what you will do and share it with the group. When choosing a group action, determine who will take responsibility for different aspects of the action. The following are secondary suggestions:

1. Provide support for someone who is having difficulty coping with the many unexpected turns in life.

2. Become a member of a support group that is helping people walk through some difficult passage in life such as the death of a loved one or loss of any kind.

3. Suggest a group discussion around a book or article that has helped any member of your group grow in their understanding of who God is and how God acts in our midst.

4. Read the Book of Job in the Old Testament and learn from the insights gathered in that encounter with God. Write down your own insights.

Invitation to Closing Prayer

Give thanks to God (aloud or silently) for insights gained, for desires awakened, for directions clarified, for the gift of one another's openness and sensitivity. Conclude with the following:

O most loving God and gentle Father,
you are the source of all wisdom and knowledge.

We thank you for all your gifts to us, most especially
the gift of your risen Son present in our midst.

We pray that we may grow daily in our understanding
of your love and your presence.

Help us to see with eyes of faith and to go deeper into
our understanding of your love and action in our midst.

May our seeing continually develop and improve.

We ask this through the power of your risen Son
and the Holy Spirit.

Amen

Second Sunday of Easter

Forgiveness of Neighbour

Invitation to Pray

Pause for a few moments of silence and enter more deeply into the presence of God.

> *Song:* "We Walk by Faith," Henry Alford &
> Marty Haugen, GIA

> *Proclaim the gospel:* John 20:19-31
> Jesus Appears to His Disciples
> behind Locked Doors

Take a few minutes to savour a word, a phrase, a question, or a feeling that rises up in you. Reflect on this quietly or share it aloud. (The other Scripture readings of the day are Acts 4:32-35 and 1 John 5:1-6.)

Invitation to Reflect on the Gospel

Jesus appears in the very midst of fear – doors closed and locked. He enters and embraces all who are there with the greeting of peace that he offers several times.

How often are we like the disciples? Do we lock ourselves up in fear and refuse to go out? Even more deadly, how often do we refuse to let anyone in? That is ultimately what creates separation and breakdown of relationships – when we are afraid to go out and when we fear to let others enter.

Reconciliation requires that we break down the boundaries that separate and divide. Then we will indeed experience the peace (shalom implies wholeness and the welfare of all as well as absence of conflict) that Jesus comes to offer completely, totally and freely.

In order for peace and reconciliation to occur, we have to be willing, like Jesus, to show our wounds, our vulnerability, our brokenness. This is the path to forgiveness and reconciliation. I must admit that I have pain and weaknesses that I have confronted and continue to deal with, yet I cannot do it alone. I need the help of others, and reconciliation is the first step toward that.

Through the sacrament of holy orders the priest receives the power to forgive sins through the sacrament of reconciliation. However, the responsibility of being about the work of reconciliation extends beyond Jesus and those to whom he has granted special powers. By our baptismal call, the whole community is to be in tune with the Spirit and freely choose to take on the mind and heart of Christ.

That community is constantly seeking means to forgive others, as well as avenues of asking for forgiveness of those it has offended or hurt. It is not the community who withholds forgiveness. Only those who close themselves off from the power of the reconciling Spirit in their lives will refuse the gift of reconciliation. They will, therefore, find it difficult to be part of this reconciling 'shalom' community. They will not allow themselves a part in the open and vulnerable stance of this Spirit-led group. Each follower of Christ is baptismally called to exercise this ministry of reconciliation and forgiveness. It is at the heart of Jesus' ministry. It is the very foundation of community.

This is not an easy ministry and we cannot enter into it lightly. We often fight this call to reconciliation and forgiveness because it not only means we have to change, but also we have to be open to be changed by others. Left to ourselves, this would be an insurmountable task. That is why the gift of the Holy Spirit in our midst is essential to our ministry. That is why the Spirit is so intimately linked to this baptismal call, this ministry of reconciliation.

Invitation to Group Sharing

1. Relate an experience of reconciliation in your life. What were the lessons I learned from that experience? In what way was the sacrament of reconciliation a part of the experience?

2. How do I separate myself from others and refuse to let others in?

3. How do I reach out to others, willing to display my own wounds and my own brokenness?

4. How do I join with others in my Church community to create an atmosphere of peace, reconciliation, and forgiveness, enabling all to feel welcome?

Invitation to Act

Determine a specific action (individual or group) that flows from your sharing. This should be your primary consideration. When choosing an individual action, determine what you will do and share it with the group. When choosing a group action, determine who will take responsibility for different aspects of the action. The following are secondary suggestions:

1. Recall how long it has been since you received the sacrament of reconciliation. Resolve to celebrate the sacrament in the next week or two.

2. Find a person this week that you need to ask forgiveness of and do so.

3. Be open and receptive to someone who has asked forgiveness of you, especially if you find it difficult to forgive and be reconciled to that person.

4. Name three things you plan to do to practice the ministry of reconciliation in your family context.

Invitation to Closing Prayer

Give thanks to God (aloud or silently) for insights gained, for desires awakened, for directions clarified, for the gift of one another's openness and sensitivity. Conclude with the following:

Leader	Spirit of love, peace and truth, we ask you to hear our prayer and grant us your peace.
Response	Graciously hear us, O Lord.
Leader	Merciful God, help us to forgive, we pray...R
Leader	Creative God, help us to arrive at innovative solutions to our conflicts, we pray...R
Leader	Gracious God, grant peace and harmony to those we have caused pain, we pray...R
Leader	Loving God, give us the strength to reach out to those we have hurt, we pray...R
Leader	Compassionate God, allow us to model our compassion on yours, we pray...R

Leader   God of unity, break down the walls that divide,
and help us to form community
wherever we go, we pray…R

Leader   Spirit of love, peace, and truth, be with us.
Strengthen us for the ministry of healing.
Be with us in love and in hope.
We ask all this through Christ our Lord.

All   Amen

Third Sunday of Easter

Witness of Christ Dying and Rising from the Dead

Invitation to Pray

Pause for a few moments of silence and enter more deeply into the presence of God.

> ***Song:*** "Bread of Life, Hope of the World,"
> Bernadette Farrell, OCP

> ***Proclaim the gospel:*** Luke 24:35-48
> Jesus Appears to His Disciples and
> Eats with Them

Take a few minutes to savour a word, a phrase, a question, or a feeling that rises up in you. Reflect on this quietly or share it aloud. (The other Scripture readings of the day are Acts 3:13-15, 17-19 and 1 John 2:1-5a.)

Invitation to Reflect on the Gospel

In order to witness effectively to God, we must first have faith in God. Faith demands that we turn our minds and hearts over to this relationship with God in our everyday lives. Without this process, witnessing is not really possible. What are some of the elements of our faith in God's loving presence?

Like the disciples, we must come in contact with the person of Jesus on a variety of levels. The most significant and important level is that of experiencing the risen Jesus alive and present in our midst. This is not a figment of our imagination but a living reality that can only be perceived with the eyes of faith. Like the disciples in this reading, we have to be open to seeing with new eyes how Christ is present and operative in our everyday lives.

Our seeing is enhanced, focused, and sharpened constantly by sharing at the table of the Lord and by continually reflecting on the Word of the Lord as given to us in Scripture. Both forms of encounter will continually confront us with the reality of dying and rising, and with the fact that rising is only possible after death has been faced and embraced.

Only when we have engaged effectively with these realities can we truly go forth to witness as followers of Christ. True witnessing and discipleship consistently requires dying to self and rising to and in Christ. This has to be the model in our lives for others.

The term martyr comes from the Greek word for witness. At times, witnessing demands that all be given up for the sake of the faith, even one's very life. Thus martyrdom has consistently been associated with witnessing to one's faith, beliefs, and values to the point of death.

Like the Master, we, too, are called, if necessary, to witness to the point of death. This is not an easy road to travel. Few seek this road with enthusiasm and eagerness. Yet, if necessary, what would be our response to such a call?

The best form of witnessing is with our lives and by our example. Others should be able to see in our lifestyle and in our relationships that Jesus' gospel values are alive and operative in our lives. It is the best way to witness the risen Christ in our midst. We are truly Christ to all we encounter. How do we measure up?

Invitation to Group Sharing

1. To whom or to what group could I do a better job of witnessing to Christ? How will I go about this?

2. How do I continually nourish my witnessing to the risen Lord at the eucharistic table and at the encounter with the living Word of God in the Scriptures?

3. Who have been my models of effective witnessing to the risen Christ? What characteristics did they exhibit, and what have I learned from them?

4. Name a time when witnessing to Christ has cost our parish community dearly. If we cannot name one, what does this say about our parish community as an effective witness to the dying and risen Christ? How can we be more effective witnesses?

Invitation to Act

Determine a specific action (individual or group) that flows from your sharing. This should be your primary consideration. When choosing an individual action, determine what you will do and share it with the group. When choosing a group action, determine who will take responsibility for different aspects of the action. The following are secondary suggestions:

1. Personally affirm the witness of others by telling them of the great model of faith they have been to you.

2. Determine ways in which you will better witness to your family and friends.

3. Become familiar with individuals or groups who are

contemporary martyrs for the faith. Work toward alleviating the plight of those who suffer greatly for their faith.

4. Together watch the movie, "Romero," and discuss its lessons and implications for how we are to witness to the risen Christ in our midst. The film can be obtained from good Catholic bookshops or www.amazon.co.uk

Invitation to Closing Prayer

Give thanks to God (aloud or silently) for insights gained, for desires awakened, for directions clarified, for the gift of one another's openness and sensitivity. Conclude with the following:

Risen Lord, we come before you, grateful
for the total gift of self that you have so freely given.

This gift cost you greatly.

Yet, you willingly gave so we might learn what it means
to live a life truly in tune with the Father's will and intention.

We ask you to send forth the power of your Spirit, to
strengthen us to be effective witnesses to your dying
and rising.

Help us to give without hesitation, even if it will cost us
dearly.

Help us to trust that all will work out well if we are faithful
to witnessing what it means to be truly human,
people full of dignity and great worth.

We ask this through the power of your Spirit. Amen

Fourth Sunday of Easter

Good Shepherding

Invitation to Pray

Pause for a few moments of silence and enter more deeply into the presence of God.

> *Song:* "Because the Lord is my Shepherd,"
> Christopher Walker, OCP

> *Proclaim the gospel:* John 10:11-18
> Jesus, the Good Shepherd

Take a few minutes to savour a word, a phrase, a question, or a feeling that rises up in you. Reflect on this quietly or share it aloud. (The other Scripture readings of the day are Acts 4:8-12 and 1 John 3:1-2.)

Invitation to Reflect on the Gospel

This chapter from John's Gospel is so important that a section of it is proclaimed in every cycle of the *Lectionary*. It focuses on Jesus as the model of the Good Shepherd. John touches on several aspects of good shepherding. Let us look at a few of those.

The primary purpose of a shepherd is to care for the needs of the sheep and to make sure they are protected from threats of any kind. The shepherd knows better than the sheep exactly what is needed and how to provide for them. Throughout our history, we have called our designated Church leaders – our pastors – shepherds. Even the symbol of the shepherd's staff is still utilized by bishops to represent their key function of protecting and attending to the needs of all under their care. In the time when most people did not attend school, the priest or bishop was usually the most educated person in the area. Therefore, he often had more knowledge and insight into life's situations. People depended on him for leadership, which could dictate what needed to happen, based on this education and wisdom.

This required a great trust by the people in their pastors. It also demanded honesty and the purest of intentions of pastors. Pastors were to guide with nothing but the good of all the people in mind. They were to make sure their actions were not tainted by seeking after ambition, power, wealth or status. The pastor had to know his people well, be able to represent them, and speak for them whenever necessary. Laying down one's life for them was the ultimate sacrifice that a shepherd could do for those under his care.

But what of a flock that is educated, at times as much as or more than the pastor? What kind of shepherding is required then? The need is still there, but it takes on an expanded role and understanding. While maintaining a distinctive prophetic, teaching, and governance role, the pastor is on a common journey with the people, trying to discern together ways in which God is calling us. Leadership or shepherding requires a sense of mutual listening and discerning. In the end, the Pope and bishops have a charism (special gift of the Holy Spirit) and responsibility to express the Church's teaching. How do we work together to carry out Jesus' mission in our present day and age?

We, the pilgrim people of God, continually search for such answers as we journey together with our shepherd. Each brings unique talents, gifts, and wisdom to the journey. Together, we discern God's call and God's viewpoint. Together, we try to articulate and model that mission in our everyday lives.

Both pastor and people are to know one another. We have to be willing both to accept and be challenged by the perspective that the other brings to the journey of the pilgrim people of God. The shepherd's role involves fidelity to the tradition and a call to teach and invoke that heritage in any process of discernment. We do this under the guidance and inspiration of the Spirit, who is ever ready to grant wisdom, discernment, and gentle guidance as we struggle to articulate Jesus' mission for our day and time.

Invitation to Group Sharing

1. How do we continually nourish ourselves as we attempt to discern the direction of our journey as members of this particular community of faith?

2. How do I work together with my priest to discern God's will for our parish community?

3. In what ways can I, or we, encourage others to use their gifts?

4. When and how do I offer my gifts and talents to further the mission and ministry of my parish community? In what new ways can I continue to do this?

Invitation to Act

Determine a specific action (individual or group) that flows from your sharing. This should be your primary consideration. When choosing an individual action, determine what you will do and share it with the group. When choosing a group action, determine who will take responsibility for different aspects of the action. The following are secondary suggestions:

1. To be a good shepherd requires good stewardship of time, talent, and treasure. With others in the parish community, help set up a process that takes seriously the many gifts and talents available, matching those talents and gifts to ministerial needs around your parish.

2. Make time as a group to get to know your priest by inviting him to your faith sharing. Ask him to share his hopes and dreams for the parish community, as you also share yours with him.

3. Discover what your Diocese is doing to develop the ministry of the laity.

Invitation to Closing Prayer

Give thanks to God (aloud or silently) for insights gained, for desires awakened, for directions clarified, for the gift of one another's openness and sensitivity. Conclude with the following:

O loving Spirit of wisdom and light,
be with us as we call upon you.

Grant us the sight needed to perceive the many gifts and talents you have abundantly bestowed upon us.

Open our hearts that we may generously share with everyone, all that you have given us.

Gently and continually nudge us in the direction of being signs of your presence and power, rather than our own.

Be with us always,
as we place ourselves into your guiding hands.

We ask this through Christ, our Lord.

Amen

Fifth Sunday of Easter

The Vine and Branches Together Bear Fruit

Invitation to Pray

Pause for a few moments of silence and enter more deeply into the presence of God.

> *Song:* "Unless a Grain of Wheat," Bernadette Farrell, OCP

> *Proclaim the gospel:* John 15:1-8
> The Vine and the Branches

Take a few minutes to savour a word, a phrase, a question, or a feeling that rises up in you. Reflect on this quietly or share it aloud. (The other Scripture readings of the day are Acts 9:26-31 and 1 John 3:18-24.)

Invitation to Reflect on the Gospel

The reality of this passage is borne out in the everyday experience of tending grape vines. Before the sap starts to rise in the vine, the first pruning has to occur. All the dead branches need to be removed and excess branches are trimmed back. As the sap rises in the vine and new sets of branches begin to develop, a second pruning occurs. Since too many branches begin to grow, some have to be pruned off so that the life of the vine is channelled to the remaining branches. This second pruning assures that the fruit is more abundant, richer, sweeter, and bigger. It is only by working together in a coordinated effort, greatly aided by the "vine grower," that vine and branches can produce at all.

We, as Christians, cannot grow without attachment to the vine, that is, to Jesus Christ, and we must accept that reality. But that is not enough. We must be willing to be pruned, to be open to conversion if we are to bear fruit and bear it abundantly. Don't forget that this pruning may frequently occur in everyday setbacks, sickness, and humbling experiences.

The intimacy of the connection between vine and branches cannot be underestimated. It is this closeness that leads to abundant fruit. This intimacy involves a willingness on our part to be attached to the vine. This is often hard for us because we desire freedom and independence, rather than what appears at first sight to be dependence and lack of freedom. To have our very being depend on our attachment to Jesus, who is the vine, calls for great faith on our part. And yet, this is what is required if we are to bear fruit. The vine without the braches cannot bring forth fruit. Yet without the vine, the branches have no life and no existence. "Unless the LORD build the house, they labour in vain who build" (Psalm 127:1). The intimacy and attachment of both vine and branches are needed if sweet, abundant, and delicious fruit is to be produced.

Intimacy involves risk. It requires willingness to be vulnerable and open to the possibility of being changed and influenced by others. It requires constant change, along with a constant, dynamic process of conversion. The language of pruning is appropriate here because pruning is not a one-off activity. It is an ongoing process with the purpose of bearing fruit that will give life. Intimacy and growth involve continual conversion, continual dying to self so that we might have life, and have it more abundantly.

Invitation to Group Sharing

1. How willing am I to be dependent on others in order to maintain and sustain life in all of its many dimensions?

2. What are some of the ways I have been pruned by the God, the 'vine grower'? In what ways do I now need to be pruned? What thoughts and feelings surfaced for me as I was going through the experience?

3. How will I show my willingness to take risks in working with God and others so that good fruit may result from our relationship?

4. What can we do to help one another walk through the struggle required for conversion and pruning to take place?

Invitation to Act

Determine a specific action (individual or group) that flows from your sharing. This should be your primary consideration. When choosing an individual action, determine what you will do and share it with the group. When choosing a group action, determine who will take responsibility for different aspects of the action. The following are secondary suggestions:

1. Name a relationship you need to work on because you have allowed it to become lifeless. Do whatever pruning is required so that new life and richer fruit can result. This might be with God and others.

2. Risk reaching out to others with whom you have no desire to or are unwilling to develop a relationship. Even if it proves to be difficult, try all that you can to maintain the link. Be open to being changed as a result.

3. Examine the relationships within your family. Make a list of the things you do that are life-giving and the things you do that are not. Work on strengthening the former and minimizing the latter.

4. Look at your wider neighbourhood and community and determine a place, situation, or group that could benefit from new life and new resources. Decide how you, as a group, can be life-giving to that particular context or situation.

Invitation to Closing Prayer

Give thanks to God (aloud or silently) for insights gained, for desires awakened, for directions clarified, for the gift of one another's openness and sensitivity. Conclude with the following:

O most loving and gracious Father,

intimacy, change, pruning, conversion,
are all such difficult processes to enter into
that we often shy away from them,
or deny the fact we are in need of them.

Grant us the courage to enter into these necessary steps
required for human relationship and growth.

Help us to realise once again that while these things for us
at times, seem almost impossible,
with you all things are possible.

Send forth upon us
your Spirit of courage, wisdom, and power,
and may your Spirit guide us in the difficult paths
we find hard to walk.

We do all this so that we might continue to be
sources of life for ourselves
and for all we encounter.

We ask this through your Son Jesus
and in the power of the Holy Spirit. Amen

Sixth Sunday of Easter

Call to Mission and Ministry

Invitation to Pray

Pause for a few moments of silence and enter more deeply into the presence of God.

> *Song:* "A New Commandment," Author Unknown

> *Proclaim the gospel:* John 15:9-17
> The Command to Go Forth and
> Love One Another

Take a few minutes to savour a word, a phrase, a question, or a feeling that rises up in you. Reflect on this quietly or share it aloud. (The other Scripture readings of the day are Acts 10:25-26, 34-35, 44-48 and 1 John 4:7-10.)

Invitation to Reflect on the Gospel

This reading is set in the context of John's long Last Supper discourse, which is Jesus' farewell address to his disciples. It offers support, encouragement, challenge, and direction for continuing the mission once Jesus is no longer physically present.

Jesus offers himself as the example upon which ministry is to be modelled. That model was first manifested in the Father's relationship to Jesus, and by extension, Jesus' relationship to us. The heart of this consists in reaching out in love and concern to all, giving even to the point of death. "No one has greater love than this" (John 15:13) is the very foundation of ministry.

This can only be accomplished in and through the intimacy we are called to by Jesus: "I have called you friends, because I have told you everything I have heard from my Father" (John 15:15). That intimacy has to be consistently cultivated if we are ever to go out in mission and be of service to others. We cannot do it on our own. It is the Lord's work, accomplished in and through the power of the Spirit.

The key word that needs to be stressed in this passage is the word "remain." Falling in love or establishing a friendship is one thing. This sometimes happens quickly. It is more difficult to develop and sustain that friendship or love relationship over an extended time. That is the challenge given to us, to "remain" in God's love as expressed in the person of Jesus.

The call to friendship with Jesus demands a reciprocal response from us. This friendship enables us to approach and enter into that knowledge of what God desires, and what we, in turn, are called to do. The insights gained from this friendship will be the very heart of ministry. We are fed on this intimacy and then sent forth to carry out that same mission, that same call to intimacy with others. This is not easy, for it will sometimes result in rejection and misunderstanding. It will call for great, or possibly even total sacrifice.

How do we accomplish this call to mission? We do it in fidelity to the call to love one another. The intimacy with Jesus has been first offered to us. This intimacy compels us to share the mission with others. The mission of Jesus – and our corresponding mission and ministry – is to love one another. In the baptismal call, we take on the mind and heart of Jesus. We enter a community that publicly commits itself to remain in God's love and to share that love with all whom we encounter.

Invitation to Group Sharing

1. In what ministry or outreach am I involved? What led me to that ministry or outreach and what causes me to "remain" in it?

2. What have been the moments when "remaining" has been difficult and challenging for me? In what ways did I sense God's call to move on or stay?

3. How do I overcome the obstacles that challenge my engagement in ministry to give all, even to the point of death?

4. How personally do we instill that discipline to "remain" in ourselves, and how do we instill that in others, especially those who come after us, either in our families or our parish communities?

Invitation to Act

Determine a specific action (individual or group) that flows from your sharing. This should be your primary consideration. When choosing an individual action, determine what you will do and share it with the group. When choosing a group action, determine who will take responsibility for different aspects of the action. The following are secondary suggestions:

1. Examine your gifts and talents and determine what ministry can best use them. If you are already involved in too many ministries, focus your attention on what you are best gifted for and place all your efforts and attention there.

2. Attend days of reflection with people in similar ministries in order to refresh and renew the intimacy with God required for any and all ministry. If there are none available, suggest one or gather a group who would be willing to work on developing such a time of reflection and renewal.

3. Develop a strategy for cultivating ministry among young people, starting with your own family, as well as with your parish family. Search out ways in which young people can minister and then invite them to get involved in the ministry, guiding and supporting them along the way.

Invitation to Closing Prayer

Give thanks to God (aloud or silently) for insights gained, for desires awakened, for directions clarified, for the gift of one another's openness and sensitivity. Conclude with the following:

Loving Father, we thank you for the many gifts
you have showered upon us in and through
the abundant manifestation of your Spirit.

You inspired Saint Paul to write that,

"There are different kinds of spiritual gifts but the same Spirit;
there are different forms of service but the same Lord;
there are different workings but the same God
who produces all of them in everyone.
To each individual the manifestation of the Spirit
is given for some benefit".

We ask for the wisdom to realise that our gifts are given for the common good and for helping others to live in your kingdom.

Make us good stewards of our gifts,
manifesting them whenever and wherever needed.

Always be with us in our challenge
to "remain" in relationship with others, for it is your love and grace that will sustain us always in our ministry.

We ask this through your Son and in the Holy Spirit.
Amen

The Ascension of the Lord

Believing in Goodness

Invitation to Pray

Pause for a few moments of silence and enter more deeply into the presence of God.

> *Song:* "I Will Be With You," Gerald Markland,
> Kevin Mayhew Ltd

> *Proclaim the gospel:* Mark 16:15-20
> Jesus' Mission Leads to the
> Goodness of the Lord

Take a few minutes to savour a word, a phrase, a question, or a feeling that rises up in you. Reflect on this quietly or share it aloud. (The other Scripture readings of the day are Acts 1:1-11 and Ephesians 4:1-13.)

Invitation to Reflect on the Gospel

The great emphasis of this passage is on sending forth the disciples to proclaim the gospel and to do great and marvellous deeds in the name of Jesus. It orientates believers towards a view of the world that is in the hands of God. Being in the hands of God, the world is thus consistently suffused with goodness and with his care and compassion.

This has been the positive message of Mark's whole Gospel. The reign of God was made definitive with the coming of Jesus, but is not yet fulfilled. A key component of God's reign is the defeat of the evil one and triumph of good over evil. This is already assured in the Resurrection of Jesus and in his ultimate triumph over the power of sin and death. Thus, for believers in Jesus, goodness already triumphs and will be evident to all who believe. In that faith stance, believers will be able to work marvels and wonders, for it is the Lord who operates in and through them.

This belief in the goodness of all creation and in the mighty deeds that will be accomplished is not a naive, untested belief. Just as Jesus experienced opposition, resistance, misunderstanding and rejection, he will continually accompany anyone who responds in faith and belief to that goodness present in our midst. Resurrection, glory, and triumph of goodness come at a steep price, the price of the cross. The cross is integral to following Jesus. Are we ready and willing to pay the price so that goodness continues to become more evident and more real?

Faith enables us to believe in the goodness of all already evident in the world, thanks to Jesus. Lack of belief paralyses us, miring us in the inability to perceive the goodness of all God's creation. The choice is ours. That will determine whether or not others will see God's goodness operative in the world or will be left in darkness. What will be our choice?

Invitation to Group Sharing

1. How have I tried consistently to take on the view that God's presence and power suffuse the world with goodness and love?

2. What can I do to instill this goodness perspective in others? What strategies can I put into place so I will consistently react naturally in stressing God's goodness in the world?

3. What can we, as a group, do to emphasise the fact that God's love and power are truly in charge of the world? When events and happenings seem to say

otherwise, how can we highlight the faith perspective, and bring God's light to the apparent dark mindset that might prevail?

Invitation to Act

Determine a specific action (individual or group) that flows from your sharing. This should be your primary consideration. When choosing an individual action, determine what you will do and share it with the group. When choosing a group action, determine who will take responsibility for different aspects of the action. The following are secondary suggestions:

1. When looking at the world around you, always put on your 'goodness' lenses. This will, at times, demand great faith and a looking beyond mere appearances. Develop strategies to consistently cultivate such a worldview.

2. Seek out people and groups who do things for others just out of the goodness of their hearts without any ulterior motives. Talk to them about what motivates them. Try to make that mindset your own.

3. Get in touch with a prison chaplain or a hospital chaplain, whichever setting suits your gifts or interest. Become part of a team that ministers to those in hospitals or prisons. People in both settings are often shunned because of the difficulty of seeing God's goodness in them, their human dignity, or worth.

4. Volunteer time at a homeless shelter or minister alongside those who give support to those who are homeless. Seek to affirm constantly the dignity of every human being, no matter how smelly, sick, or unapproachable for whatever reason.

Invitation to Closing Prayer

Give thanks to God (aloud or silently) for insights gained, for desires awakened, for directions clarified, for the gift of one another's openness and sensitivity. Conclude with the following:

> Blessed are you, Lord God of all creation
> and Father of us all, for the gift of your Son
> who has shown us what it means to be human.
>
> His presence in our midst infinitely ennobles our
> human dignity and worth beyond anything imaginable.
>
> We thank and praise you for that magnificent gift.
>
> Like your Son, let us walk among one another as your
> sons and daughters, members of the same family.
>
> Let us always affirm the dignity and worth of every
> human being, and give us the grace and the strength
> when such affirmation is difficult for us.
>
> We ask this through your Son, Jesus,
> and in the Holy Spirit. Amen

Seventh Sunday of Easter

Consecrated to Truth

Invitation to Pray

Pause for a few moments of silence and enter more deeply into the presence of God.

> *Song:* "Love Divine, All Loves Excelling,"
> Charles Wesley

> *Proclaim the gospel:* John 17:11b-19
> Jesus' Prayer for His Disciples

Take a few minutes to savour a word, a phrase, a question, or a feeling that rises up in you. Reflect on this quietly or share it aloud. (The other Scripture readings of the day are Acts 1:15-17, 20a, 20c-26 and 1 John 4:11-16.)

Invitation to Reflect on the Gospel

This gospel comes from a chapter of John usually referred to as Jesus' high priestly prayer. It is Jesus' final prayer and last statement in John's Gospel before he is arrested and killed. It is a prayer offered to the Father in the name of those Jesus has called to be his disciples.

The section's significance stems from the fact that Jesus realises if the disciples take up his mission and ministry they will experience, just as he did, persecution, rejection, misunderstanding, and opposition. When Jesus experienced such realities, he stayed the course and continued to proclaim God's truth and intention without compromise and without hesitation. This reality is at the heart of the command: "As I have loved you, so you also should love one another" (John 13:34). Jesus continues to be the model upon which this commandment must take shape.

This is what Jesus means when asking God the Father to consecrate his disciples in truth. God's Word and God's action are truth. Jesus is living in truth and is a model for them. Jesus is asking the same for them as he returns to the Father. They are to go forth and be living examples of God to all they encounter. As a result, this dedication and commitment to truth becomes a key source of joy and contentment in the disciples' lives.

To be consecrated to truth involves commitment and determination not to compromise or hesitate in proclaiming the truth loudly and clearly, no matter what the consequences. It may demand a great deal to take this stance for truth. The opposition from all sides will be a living reality that has to be continually addressed. It will bring all sorts of unpleasantness and even threats to our lives. Some may even be called to give all for the sake of the truth. This is difficult and harsh to comprehend. Yet Jesus asks the Father to protect all who would be consecrated to truth.

Just as Jesus has proclaimed that truth to us, we are to proclaim that truth to and for one another. Thus, one of the true marks of discipleship is being committed to truth, consecrating one's whole life and being to proclaiming the reality and truth that God is love. Let us continue to consecrate ourselves daily to truth and make Jesus' prayer a lived reality in our midst.

Invitation to Group Sharing

1. In what specific ways in my life have I consecrated myself to truth and to testifying in truth?

2. As a disciple of Jesus what would I want my final prayer and last statement to be?

3. How do I deal with rejection and misunderstanding, especially when the truth I speak is twisted into something foreign, strange, and inaccurate?

Invitation to Act

Determine a specific action (individual or group) that flows from your sharing. This should be your primary consideration. When choosing an individual action, determine what you will do and share it with the group. When choosing a group action, determine who will take responsibility for different aspects of the action. The following are secondary suggestions:

1. Every time you are tempted to twist the truth or tell little white lies resist the temptation and speak honestly. Make sure you do this for yourself, but most especially for young people who may see you as their role model, or who are just observing you for some reason.

2. Write letters to your elected representatives urging them to speak the truth on every issue they encounter and not to twist the facts for the sake of public policy, political gain or pressure from interest groups.

3. As a group, affirm and rejoice in the telling of the truth in all sorts of structures and people, especially in young people. Support, write letters of affirmation, tell others you interact with, and celebrate the fact that truth has prevailed even if it means sacrifice, hardship, or other realities.

4. Spend time in prayerful reflection writing what you would want your final prayer to be. Share it with a close friend or family member.

Invitation to Closing Prayer

Give thanks to God (aloud or silently) for insights gained, for desires awakened, for directions clarified, for the gift of one another's openness and sensitivity. Conclude with the following:

Leader   Loving God, we have reflected
on what it means to be consecrated to truth.
We pray for all your human family
that we may all be dedicated to truth and love.

Leader   For all of us, that we may truly be models to all,
especially our young people, of what it means
to be consecrated to truth, we pray...

Response   O Lord, consecrate all to truth.

Leader   For all the times we have affirmed and rejoiced
in the truth, we pray...R

Leader   For all those who find truth difficult to sustain,
that we may encourage and support them as we
all struggle to proclaim the truth, we pray...R

Leader   For all the times we have failed to be consecrated
to truth, we pray...R

Leader   For all leaders, that in leading, they lead with
dedication to truth no matter what the cost, we
pray...R

Leader   Hear our prayers, Lord,
as you heard the prayer of your Son.
We ask this in his name and in the Holy Spirit.

All   Amen

Pentecost Sunday

Community: A Gift of the Holy Spirit

Invitation to Pray

Pause for a few moments of silence and enter more deeply into the presence of God.

> ***Song:*** "Come down, O Love Divine," Bianco di Siena, tr. R Littledale

> ***Proclaim the gospel:*** John 15:26-27; 16:12-15
> The Spirit of Truth Will Guide You

Take a few minutes to savour a word, a phrase, a question, or a feeling that rises up in you. Reflect on this quietly or share it aloud. (The other Scripture readings of the day are Acts 2:1-11 and Galatians 5:16-25.)

Invitation to Reflect on the Gospel

This passage, taken from Jesus' farewell discourse to his disciples at the Last Supper is one of several in John's Gospel devoted to the role and function of the Paraclete, a Greek word meaning "one who calls alongside of another." Jesus is preparing his disciples for the fact that he will soon no longer be with them. He has worked with them and prepared them as much as possible, and he is not leaving them orphans. Jesus promises that when he is gone, he will send another Paraclete (John 14:16), the Holy Spirit, one who will be a source of comfort to them, as well as an advocate and a guide.

This Advocate is the Spirit of truth who will testify and witness to Jesus and all that he has done and said while he walked on earth. Not only will the Spirit testify to what the disciples have already experienced but also to things they have yet to face, namely Jesus' passion, death, and Resurrection. In all this, the Spirit of truth will be a teacher, a guide, and a helper. The Spirit of truth will continue what Jesus has begun, leading his followers to an ever deeper understanding of Jesus' person and his relation to the Father and to further insight into Jesus' work and teachings.

The Holy Spirit's role is essential to each and every follower of Jesus. Without the Spirit's presence as a teacher, guide, and advocate, we, along with all disciples, would be left alone, lacking insight and wisdom. It is the guidance and inspiration of the Holy Spirit that activate our own witnessing to Jesus, leading us to live, teach, and hand on the truth of the faith to others. Without such assurance and reliance, we would soon lose our way and not remain in the truth of Jesus.

The Holy Spirit is given to all who align themselves as disciples of Jesus, not just to a privileged few. Thus all who have been baptised, born from above of water and the Holy Spirit (John 3:5), have received the Spirit, as their assurance and guide to the truth in the midst of uncertainty and limitations. It is our responsibility to attune ourselves to the Spirit's presence and guidance. We need to discern the voice and actions of the Holy Spirit, functioning in the Church on behalf of the world. We need to pay attention to the 'signs of the times' in the light of the gospel message so that we can learn where the Spirit is guiding us. Developing a deep understanding of the Church's teaching and a life of prayer attuned to the Scriptures will enable us to discern the presence and action of the Spirit in our world. In this fashion, we are led by the Spirit and we witness to, glorify, and continually explore and develop our relationship with Jesus, and thus with God the Father.

Invitation to Group Sharing

1. How do I attune myself to the action and movement of the Holy Spirit in my world: for myself, my family, my community, my work, our Church?

2. How do I continually work on developing a spirituality that is attuned to the action of the Holy Spirit in my life, making me more adept at discerning the witnessing, teaching, and guiding work of the Spirit?

3. How do we, as a community of Jesus' disciples, witness to the great and marvellous deeds that God the Father, in the person of Jesus and through the power of the Holy Spirit, continually accomplishes in our midst? How can we be enduring witnesses of these deeds?

Invitation to Act

Determine a specific action (individual or group) that flows from your sharing. This should be your primary consideration. When choosing an individual action, determine what you will do and share it with the group. When choosing a group action, determine who will take responsibility for different aspects of the action. The following are secondary suggestions:

1. If you are not already, become part of a small Christian community that is trying to connect faith with everyday life. Seek its support in building sensitivity to the work of the Holy Spirit in our midst, especially as focused in our parish communities, families, and careers. If there are no small Christian communities in your parish, seek out ways to start one.

2. Respond to the prompting of the Holy Spirit by writing letters, e-mails, and praying for an end to the many injustices evident in our world. These could include an end to the death penalty, working toward nonviolent resolutions to resolve conflicts, working against the persistent evils of racism and sexism. Discern other areas of injustice with your faith community and together strive to witness to the values of Jesus.

3. Witness to and glorify God's truth and blessings in your midst by celebrating the many different gifts and the cultural diversity present in your community. Celebrate the Eucharist in a different cultural community than you normally do. Actively participate in diocesan celebrations that affirm the cultural, ethnic, and social diversity that exists in the wider Church community.

4. Actively take part in groups that are working toward establishing peace and harmony throughout the world, such as those working for peace in areas of conflict.

5. Try to make contact with your parish/Diocesan Justice & Peace group. See what you can do together in partnership.

Invitation to Closing Prayer

Give thanks to God (aloud or silently) for insights gained, for desires awakened, for directions clarified, for the gift of one another's openness and sensitivity. Conclude with the following:

> O gentle and warm Spirit,
> source of all truth and peace,
> be with us in a special way this day.
>
> You have showered so many
> wonderful gifts upon us, your people.
>
> Help us to grow in appreciation of the many different
> ways in which you manifest yourself in our midst.
>
> May we always pay attention to the signs of the times
> as we attune ourselves to how you speak
> in and through the splendour of all your creation.
>
> Aid us always in being sources of unity, peace, and love,
> ever sustaining life, and ever upholding the downtrodden.
>
> We ask this in the name of Jesus,
> our brother and Lord. Amen

Solemnity of the Most Holy Trinity

Teaching and Praying the Creed

Invitation to Pray

Pause for a few moments of silence and enter more deeply into the presence of God.

> ***Song:*** "We Walk by Faith," Henry Alford & Marty Haugen, GIA

> ***Proclaim the gospel:*** Matthew 28:16-20
> Jesus' Commission to His Disciples

Take a few minutes to savour a word, a phrase, a question, or a feeling that rises up in you. Reflect on this quietly or share it aloud. (The other Scripture readings of the day are Deuteronomy 4:32-34, 39-40 and Romans 8:14-17.)

Invitation to Reflect on the Gospel

These last verses of Matthew's Gospel, often referred to as the Great Commission of Jesus to his disciples, summarise all the key themes of Matthew's Gospel and serve as an appropriate ending for it.

Matthew portrays Jesus as one who teaches with authority and who can be trusted. The teaching is reliable and in line with God's intention as articulated through the Scriptures and through God's action in our midst. This teaching is reliably handed on to his followers who can also be trusted and relied upon because throughout they have understood the teaching and appropriated it into their own lives.

This teaching has been developed and articulated by the community in a verbal formula we call the Creed. It took centuries of prayer, study, and arguments before the bishops of the entire Church, meeting in council, developed the statements in our Creed. We still claim it as the summary statement of our core beliefs. It is what the mainline Christian communities pray each Sunday at liturgy and what the Church communicates in its catechetical ministry.

The heart of the Creed is the Trinitarian reality we celebrate on this day. That Trinitarian reality is the crucial glimpse we have to the mystery that is God. We pray to the Father, with the Son, in and through the power of the Spirit. We articulate who God is by looking at the reality of God in our midst, Jesus. We are guided and enlightened by Jesus' Spirit poured out throughout all of creation.

What do these glimpses suggest about our God? They suggest that God is one who already shows us what we are about, namely, people in relationship who work together to deepen and strengthen the bonds that unite us all. They also suggest that to carry this out, we need to 'do' and not just 'say.' In other words, the Trinitarian mystery prayed and taught in the Creed is the foundation for the faith that has to be lived out in everyday life, and not merely something that we mouth in prayers or in catechetical lessons. The Great Commission sends us out to teach others 'to do' all that Jesus has taught us. Let us make sure that we are "doing" what it is that we are sent out to teach. Let us 'do' and not just 'say.'

Invitation to Group Sharing

1. What significance does the Creed have in my life? How does it affect the way I think and behave?

2. What role does belief in the Trinity play in my faith life?

3. How do I plan to make the Creed a living reality in my life, rather than just something I recite?

4. What is our strategy for making the Trinity the model of what Christian community is all about? Give specific examples. How will I act on this?

Invitation to Act

Determine a specific action (individual or group) that flows from your sharing. This should be your primary consideration. When choosing an individual action, determine what you will do and share it with the group. When choosing a group action, determine who will take responsibility for different aspects of the action. The following are secondary suggestions:

1. Study the history of the Creed and how it came to be formulated. See particularly the Catechism of the Catholic Church, paragraphs 192-193.

2. Consciously pray the Creed in a group setting other than the eucharistic gathering. Then examine the meaning of each part of the Creed, and what difference that meaning makes in your life.

3. As a group, discuss how you can be a community consciously striving to make the Creed a visible sign of unity. Make a list of things that would need to happen if this is ever going to become a reality. Share that list with the parish leadership team or with the parish pastoral council.

4. Examine the areas of your life where your saying and your doing do not correspond. If you find yourself saying one thing and then doing another, focus on that. Commit yourself to making sure that for the next

month, in that particular area, your words and your actions will correspond as closely as you can make them. Then concentrate on other areas that need work. It may be difficult, so don't hesitate to ask for the Spirit's help.

Invitation to Closing Prayer

Give thanks to God (aloud or silently) for insights gained, for desires awakened, for directions clarified, for the gift of one another's openness and sensitivity. Conclude with the following:

O Most Holy Trinity, model of love and relationship, thank you for being our guide.

Your mutual love and relationship inspire and lead us.

Remind us always that constancy, persistence, and patience are the hallmarks of all relationships.

Bless us with these virtues, even when we do not seem to desire them.

Allow us to develop these virtues so that your presence is made even more manifest in our midst.

May we continue to further your reign among us, modelled on your constant love and mutual relationship.

We ask this in trust and confidence. Amen

Solemnity of the Most Holy Body and Blood of Christ

Eucharist, the Body of Christ

Invitation to Pray

Pause for a few moments of silence and enter more deeply into the presence of God.

> ***Song:*** "O Bread of Heaven," St Alphonsus Liguori, tr. Edmund Vaughan

> ***Proclaim the gospel:*** Mark 14:12-16, 22-26
> Last Supper According to Mark

Take a few minutes to savour a word, a phrase, a question, or a feeling that rises up in you. Reflect on this quietly or share it aloud. (The other Scripture readings of the day are Exodus 24:3-8 and Hebrews 9:11-15.)

Invitation to Reflect on the Gospel

Since the *Lectionary* readings of Cycle B focus on the Gospel of Mark, this is his account of the Last Supper. The Eucharist takes its significance and meaning from these actions and words of Jesus. Eucharist means 'thanksgiving' and for the early followers of Jesus the word was used as a verb and not a noun. Christians lived and gathered to do Eucharist, not to simply receive Eucharist. Eucharist was and still is the operative action that identifies, unifies, and sends out all Christians on mission for others.

For centuries Christians struggled over the meaning and significance of Christ's presence in the elements of bread and wine. They focused on the 'how' and the 'why' of that presence in those elements so that, for some, the very meaning of Eucharist is blurred. Eucharist is the action that unifies all of us as the Body of Christ. It is important to focus strongly on the real presence of Christ and also be careful to appreciate the modes of the presence of Christ in others, in the Word, in those who minister to us, and in all of creation.

The Second Vatican Council, in *The Constitution on the Sacred Liturgy* (*Sacrosanctum concilium* 7), clearly and emphatically reminds us of these many presences of Christ in the eucharistic gathering. The implications of this statement are tremendously significant. Because Christ is present in others and in the Word in modes analogous to the way he is really present in the Eucharist sacramentally, in the elements of bread and wine, then we are challenged once again to be Eucharist, the Body of Christ, and not simply to receive Eucharist. We are challenged to revere and tend to others in the same way we revere and tend to the eucharistic Christ. Christ is actively and truly present in all. When we truly act upon this belief, we move toward becoming the healing, reconciling, and unifying community that is the Mystical Body of Christ.

Taking Augustine's dictum on the Eucharist might help us focus on what we are about. About Eucharist, Augustine is attributed as saying to those gathered around the altar:
"Believe what you receive.
Receive what you believe
Become what you receive."

Invitation to Group Sharing

1. What significance is there in noting that Eucharist is a verb, that is, something the Church does, and not only a noun, that is, something I receive?

2. What meaning and significance does gathering with others around the altar have for me?

3. How do I reverence the many modes of Christ's presence in our midst, especially the modes articulated for us by the Second Vatican Council? What will I do?

Invitation to Act

Determine a specific action (individual or group) that flows from your sharing. This should be your primary consideration. When choosing an individual action, determine what you will do and share it with the group. When choosing a group action, determine who will take responsibility for different aspects of the action. The following are secondary suggestions:

1. When gathering for the Eucharist, pay attention in a special way to those who are gathering and to the stories of their lives. Learn to reverence their person and their story, as you would Jesus present in word and sacrament.

2. Reflect prayerfully on how you are Eucharist to others. Share your reflections with someone and together decide how you can more visibly be Eucharist to others.

3. Spend time before the Blessed Sacrament in loving adoration of our Lord.

4. Make a conscious effort to recognise the gifts that members of your own family bring to a daily meal. Pray together for the unity of those who gather at your table.

Invitation to Closing Prayer

Give thanks to God (aloud or silently) for insights gained, for desires awakened, for directions clarified, for the gift of one another's openness and sensitivity. Conclude with the following:

O loving God, you nourish and sustain us.
We thank you for the gift of food, which nourishes life.

You continue to be with us in so many wonderful and marvellous ways, nourishing and sustaining us always with food that gives life to all the aspects of our being.

Help us to use the many ways in which you nourish us as sources of unity and life for all of your people.

Allow us to grow in sensitivity to the plight of those who are hungry, alone, frightened, shut out, uninvited, unwelcome.

May we continually make room for them at our table, both in our homes and in our Church.

We pray this in Jesus' name
and in the power of the Holy Spirit. Amen

Season of the Year
(Ordinary Time)

Second Sunday in Ordinary Time

Vocation: "What Are You Looking For?"

Invitation to Pray

Pause for a few moments of silence and enter more deeply into the presence of God.

> *Song:* "Will You Come and Follow Me," vv 1, 2, 5, John
> Bell & Graham Maule, Wild Goose Publications

> *Proclaim the gospel:* John 1:35-42
> Come and See

Take a few minutes to savour a word, a phrase, a question, or a feeling that rises up in you. Reflect on this quietly or share it aloud. (The other Scripture readings of the day are 1 Samuel 3:3b-10, 19 and 1 Corinthians 6:13c-15a, 17-20.)

Invitation to Reflect on the Gospel

John the Baptist's role in this passage is one to which we are all called in our desire to follow Jesus. Our task is to point Jesus out to others. Then we must let go and allow them to follow Jesus in the way they feel called, not in the way we would choose. Once we have pointed out Jesus, it is their task to discern what it is they want to do. Jesus' question is at the heart of the discernment process of any vocation. As he turns around and sees them following, Jesus asks, "What are you looking for?" (John 1:38). In other words, what are the desires of your heart? To what do you feel you are being called? The response of the followers is also very interesting: "Where are you staying?" (John 1:38). They seem to ask, "Jesus, what are you all about?"

Christian vocation in life demands first and foremost a relationship with Jesus and his people in the Christian community. It is Jesus who will be able to direct us to what we are truly seeking. The call to enter into relationship with Jesus involves a search to discover our true desires. Part of that discernment is to explore all the possible avenues that are open to us, or toward which we are being pointed. What am I all about, and what is the true desire of my heart? Jesus helps us in our search to find the true answers to these questions and concerns.

Jesus offers the invitation to his disciples and to us: "Come, and you will see" (John 1:39). If you really are serious about exploring the true desires of your heart, then commit yourself to exploring what Jesus is all about. Are you willing to accept Jesus' invitation? Are you ready to embark on whatever journey that invitation demands? That invitation comes from the one who calls us into relationship – a relationship that demands openness and the possibility that we will be changed along the way.

The Documents of Vatican II spell out the vocational call in the same manner Jesus does in the gospel. Our vocational call, grounded in our baptismal commitment, is our promise to enter into relationship with Jesus and to take on the mind and heart of Jesus. There is really only one vocation, the call to holiness, the call to enter into relationship with Jesus and to model his lifestyle and values in our daily lives, no matter what we are about. This communal call to relationship with Jesus places us on a path of mutual mission, which is carried out in various lifestyles, depending on what we are attracted to and for what we discern we have gifts. Let us enter deeply into this loving relationship. Continued growth and development of this relationship are the basis and core foundation of all vocations.

Invitation to Group Sharing

1. If someone asked "Do you think you have a vocation," what would be my response, in light of my reflection on this reading?

2. When we pray as a Christian community for vocations, for what should we be praying?

3. What needs to happen if we are to continue to grow and develop in whatever vocation we perceive we have been called?

4. In what ways have I, or we, taken on the role of John the Baptist, pointing out Christ to others? How can we do this more effectively?

Invitation to Act

Determine a specific action (individual or group) that flows from your sharing. This should be your primary consideration. When choosing an individual action, determine what you will do and share it with the group. When choosing a group action, determine who will take responsibility for different aspects of the action. The following are secondary suggestions:

1. Create a prayer service for vocations, incorporating the teachings of Vatican II on the basic vocation we are all called to and the different ways we live it out. What elements would need to be emphasised so that all Christian callings in life are included?

2. Jesus asks of us, "What are you looking for?" (John 1:38). Develop a mission statement for yourself to address this question. Make sure that it includes your

deepest yearnings and desires for yourself, your family, others, and the world.

3. Jesus invites us into personal relationship with him when he says, "Come, and you will see" (John 1:39). Take time for yourself during the day to be with Jesus and develop a deeper relationship with him. Focus either on the gospel reading for the day or a psalm verse from the Liturgy of the Hours. Expand this to one hour a week, half a day a month, and even one full day a year devoted totally to developing your relationship with Christ.

4. As a group take time to share how you have consciously tried to live out your call to holiness in the lifestyle and occupation you have chosen. Give concrete examples of strategies that you have developed and of attitudes and perspectives you have cultivated to help you accomplish this goal.

Invitation to Closing Prayer

Give thanks to God (aloud or silently) for insights gained, for desires awakened, for directions clarified, for the gift of one another's openness and sensitivity. Conclude with the following:

Gentle God, loving Father, source of all goodness,
you bless us with many gifts,
most especially the gift of your Son.

Jesus invites us into loving relationship,
as he is in loving relationship with you and the Spirit.

Grant us the power of the Spirit to discern
the best way to respond to Jesus' invitation.

Give us the determination to respond
continually and fully to that call.

We ask this in and through the Christ
who calls us and the Spirit who guides us.

All praise to you Lord, now and forever.

Amen

Third Sunday in Ordinary Time

Repent and Believe

Invitation to Pray

Pause for a few moments of silence and enter more deeply into the presence of God.

> *Song:* "The Kingdom of God is Justice and Joy,"
> Bryn Rees

> *Proclaim the gospel:* Mark 1:14-20
> Repent and Believe the Good
> News

Take a few minutes to savour a word, a phrase, a question, or a feeling that rises up in you. Reflect on this quietly or share it aloud. (The other Scripture readings of the day are Jonah 3:1-5, 10 and 1 Corinthians 7:29-31.)

Invitation to Reflect on the Gospel

The first words out of Jesus' mouth in Mark's Gospel, "Repent, and believe" (Mark 1:15), become key themes of the whole gospel. Repent is a challenge to turn our lives around. Our hearts, our priorities, are to shift radically in order to open ourselves up to believe the Good News. This call demands an immediate response, especially as narrated and understood by Mark's community.

This Good News is related to the time of fulfillment. What is the Good News? What is the time of fulfillment? Mark answers that question by stressing the fact and the reality that God's very presence, in the person of Jesus, now suffuses every aspect of our lives. This active presence of God at work, constantly overcoming and defeating the forces of evil and providentially guiding all creation in Christ, establishes God's reign in all of creation, harking back to the harmony and intent of creation in Genesis.

Our first task is to recognize and acknowledge God's presence and reign in our midst. As a response to this knowledge and awareness, we are called to change our lives. Finally, we are called to believe the Good News is indeed good news for our lives. We are called to believe that evil is defeated, and that God continues to reign in our midst.

Do we truly believe this? If we truly believe it, what do we do with that awareness? How are our lives different as a result of that reality?

Another aspect of this text is the fact that any good news, most especially this most fundamental Good News, is not something to be hoarded. Of necessity, it needs to be proclaimed to all, inviting others to share in that time of fulfillment as well. Mark has Jesus call his first disciples, and us as well, to full commitment of that belief and to become full proclaimers of that Good News to all – to become fishers of all.

Mark's narrative demands a response from those who would be disciples – a response that is immediate, complete, and total. Mark symbolically communicates the fact that this call to mission and proclamation is not something that can be done with partial commitment or belief. It has to be done totally, fully, and without looking back. Existentially, that is not the way things work. Yet symbolically, for the message to eventually take hold and be proclaimed effectively, this kind of commitment and involvement is essential. Total commitment is a necessary component of true belief. With God's help, it will lead to the continual defeat of evil and the continued growth of God's presence and reign, pervading all of creation. Are we up to the task?

Invitation to Group Sharing

1. How do I understand Jesus' call to repent and believe? Repent from what and believe in what? What personal experiences give flesh to my response?

2. What does the Good News, the time of fulfillment, look like to me? What are its characteristics, and how do they compare with the characteristics Mark's Gospel delineates?

3. Do we truly believe that evil is defeated and that the reign of God suffuses all of creation? If so, what difference does this perspective make in the way we act in the world and in relation to all of creation?

4. The call to repent, believe, and proclaim the Good News to others is ours as a result of our baptismal call. How am I living out my baptismal call? How do I proclaim the Good News of God's presence in our midst to those I encounter?

Invitation to Act

Determine a specific action (individual or group) that flows from your sharing. This should be your primary consideration. When choosing an individual action, determine what you will do and share it with the group. When choosing a group action, determine who will take responsibility for different aspects of the action. The following are secondary suggestions:

1. Look at your personal and communal life and discern where a call for repentance and forgiveness is needed. Seek out the person, persons, or group affected, and ask for forgiveness. Make sure you include an explicit intention to amend your ways in the future.

2. Seek out a family member, a friend, or anyone in need of hope and good news. With your group, talk about ways you can communicate the good news of love, care, and concern to them. Develop an action plan that will effectively proclaim God's Good News to them in ways that are meaningful to their needs and concerns.

3. Work through the legal and political systems of your local government to fight crime and rid your neighbourhood of anything that smacks of hatred or inhumanity. Examples might be elimination of drug houses, countering the racist tendencies of some neighbours or some real estate people, providing safe houses for school children whose parents work, becoming part of neighbourhood watches to alert law enforcement to crime and violence.

4. Using the Rosary, pray the first Mystery of Light (Mark 1:14-15).

5. Develop or become part of your parish social action or justice and peace group as one way to proclaim effectively the Good News that God's reign is among us and that evil will no longer be tolerated in this community. Work to educate yourself and others to the rich heritage of Catholic social teaching. Do not hesitate to proclaim these principles even in the face of opposition and resistance.

Invitation to Closing Prayer

Give thanks to God (aloud or silently) for insights gained, for desires awakened, for directions clarified, for the gift of one another's openness and sensitivity. Conclude with the following:

Leader   Loving and gentle Father, for the times we have been insensitive to the needs of others...

Response   Lord, we repent and believe in the Good News.

Leader   For the times we have not resisted evil but have given in to it instead...R/

Leader   For the times we have failed to offer hope and support...R/

Leader   For the times we have shut ourselves off from comfort, hope, and support...R/

Leader   For the times we have allowed cynicism to reign...R/

Leader   Loving Father, we turn to you in love and trust. Allow your reign to grow continually in our hearts, now and always. Amen

Fourth Sunday in Ordinary Time

Recognising Goodness

Invitation to Pray

Pause for a few moments of silence and enter more deeply into the presence of God.

> *Song:* "Come to the Water," John Foley, SJ, OCP

> *Proclaim the gospel:* Mark 1:21-28
> Cure of a Demoniac

Take a few minutes to savour a word, a phrase, a question, or a feeling that rises up in you. Reflect on this quietly or share it aloud. (The other Scripture readings of the day are Deuteronomy 18:15-20 and 1 Corinthians 7:32-35.)

Invitation to Reflect on the Gospel

The people in this story were just learning who Jesus was. So they were still not seeing the amazing truth of it. However, others saw more clearly. The unclean spirits recognised him. His enemies recognised his power and were threatened by it. The centurion who saw him hanging on the cross saw and proclaimed him truly to be the Son of God (Mark 15:39). But the people closest to him, his disciples, seemed to take the longest to realise who Jesus was.

Like the disciples, each of us has some partial blindness to the truth. We carry with us a bias toward our own insights, our own views, our own opinions. Like the disciples, this can make it difficult for us to recognise what is real and true and good.

What might we learn from this? Perhaps we can learn to ask if it's typical of us not to recognise the goodness in those close to us but see it more easily in others. Is it easier for us to believe that Jesus was present to the people in the story we just read than to believe that Christ is present to us in our daily life? Like the disciples, sometimes we miss what is right before us because it is right before us. Perhaps we fail to see the talents and goodness of the people with whom we rub shoulders day after day or we stop seeing them after a while. Maybe we are blind to the presence of Christ with us in our homes, in our work, and as we move through our errands and tasks each day.

In the gospel, we see how Jesus taught the people in the synagogue on this day. First he taught by his words. Then Jesus taught by his actions. He spoke angrily to the evil one and relieved the man with the unclean spirit. Words and actions combined to make a powerful statement. Jesus is giving us an example and a challenge. We, too, are to try to match our lives, our actions, to what we say we believe.

Invitation to Group Sharing

1. To whom or what might I be blind? Are there certain people or viewpoints whose merit or goodness I cannot hear or see because of my own views or opinions? (Often, it well may be those I am very close to, for example, a family member.)

2. What is an example of someone who has taught me a lesson because his or her actions match his or her words?

3. How does our community welcome the voice of those whose viewpoints we might be slow to hear or accept?

4. Where are we showing, by what our community does, that we believe the words we profess? Where are we not doing this as well? How can we improve?

Invitation to Act

Determine a specific action (individual or group) that flows from your sharing. This should be your primary consideration. When choosing an individual action, determine what you will do and share it with the group. When choosing a group action, determine who will take responsibility for different aspects of the action. The following are secondary suggestions:

1. Continue to name for yourself people and ideas which you fail to fully recognise. Each day, say a short prayer to be open to the goodness and truth that may be there. When you are with such a person, be conscious of your desire to hear and see the truth and goodness you may be missing.

2. Choose three people who have taught you by their words and actions in the course of your life. Find an appropriate way to thank them for this.

3. In one of your community organisations, speak about your concern for times when actions seem to belie words. Do this in a way that is not accusing people, but as something you also own and are concerned about. Suggest ways to close this gap between words and actions and ask others for their thoughts and ideas on the topic. Or, as a group, decide what you can do about this together.

Invitation to Closing Prayer

Give thanks to God (aloud or silently) for insights gained, for desires awakened, for directions clarified, for the gift of one another's openness and sensitivity. Conclude with the following:

Loving God,

Jesus taught us so many lessons during his time on this earth.
As we come together to search out these lessons
we come with open hearts and minds.

Open our hearts and minds as we leave here also
that we may see the goodness you have put
in the highways and byways of our life.

Keep us attentive to your words that
our footsteps and actions may follow the same path,
the path that Jesus shows,
the path we claim to be walking.

Guide our feet that they may stay on the path of the gospel,
the way that Jesus the teacher has shown us.

We ask this through the same Christ our Lord. Amen

Fifth Sunday in Ordinary Time

Prayer and Mission

Invitation to Pray

Pause for a few moments of silence and enter more deeply into the presence of God.

> ***Song:*** "Glory and Praise to Our God," Dan Schutte, OCP

> ***Proclaim the gospel:*** Mark 1:29-39
> Cure of Simon's Mother-in-Law

Take a few minutes to savour a word, a phrase, a question, or a feeling that rises up in you. Reflect on this quietly or share it aloud. (The other Scripture readings of the day are Job 7:1-4, 6-7 and 1 Corinthians 9:16-19, 22-23.)

Invitation to Reflect on the Gospel

Once again, we see Jesus the healer at work. First he comes to the home of his hostess, Peter's mother-in-law, and heals her of the fever that has put her to bed. After sundown, when the Sabbath is ended, crowds gathered at the door for Jesus to cure many who were ill. And he did. You can imagine Jesus and the disciples must have felt exhausted after such an evening. There were crowds pressing in on them and many people, sick with various diseases, trying to come forward to him.

Then in the quiet of the next morning, Jesus slipped away to be alone to pray. He goes off to pray in the midst of busyness. This is not the only time we see such a pattern with Jesus. And what might we imagine he prayed? Perhaps prayers of thanksgiving for the goodness and blessings of the previous day;

perhaps prayers of concern for the people whom he met there; perhaps prayers for the courage and the energy to continue. Does this sound like your prayer? While we may not have days with the whole city at our door, some days it may feel that way. And when that happens we, too, are reminded by his example to take time out. We, too, need to be alone to talk with our God. We, too, need to take time to pray alone and with others.

Perhaps it was there, in the midst of that prayer, that Jesus was again clear about his mission. He goes on to spread the Good News. From town to town, he goes teaching that God calls his people and is here for them. Nothing else matters as much. This is what he came to do.

Invitation to Group Sharing

1. What are the things that prevent me from praying? What helps me overcome the obstacles? What benefits have I experienced when I have taken time to pray?

2. Jesus was clear about his mission – why he was here on earth. How would I describe my own personal mission? How can I keep that mission alive and not let it become sidetracked?

3. What are the ways our community supports the prayer life of our people with options for various styles of prayer? How might we better do that as a community?

4. How would you describe the mission of our community? What are ways we can make that mission more evident?

Invitation to Act

Determine a specific action (individual or group) that flows from your sharing. This should be your primary consideration. When choosing an individual action, determine what you will do and share it with the group. When choosing a group action, determine who will take responsibility for different aspects of the action. The following are secondary suggestions:

1. Renew your intention to pray regularly by safeguarding a special time for it.

2. Give some time to thinking about the personal mission that is yours alone. Write it down this week and list three ways you carry it out. Bring it to share next week.

3. Create a simple brochure that lists and describes the prayer opportunities your parish community provides. Share this with the entire parish. If something could be added, form a group of interested people to initiate the kind of prayer they need.

4. Reflect on the way your parish community develops its prayer life. What role can you play in this?

Invitation to Closing Prayer

Give thanks to God (aloud or silently) for insights gained, for desires awakened, for directions clarified, for the gift of one another's openness and sensitivity. Conclude with the following:

Pray slowly together

> Take away our cares that we may be present to you, O God.

Pause until a sign is given by the leader to continue

> Be with us as we open ourselves
> that we may know your presence to us, O God.

Pause until a sign is given by the leader to continue

> Flood our hearts and minds with gratitude,
> with awe and adoration, with the desire for forgiveness
> that we may commune with you, O God.

Pause until a sign is given by the leader to continue

> Our Father...

Sixth Sunday in Ordinary Time

Compassion

Invitation to Pray

Pause for a few moments of silence and enter more deeply into the presence of God.

> *Song:* "Eye Has Not Seen,"
> Marty Haugen, GIA

> *Proclaim the gospel:* Mark 1:40-45
> Cleansing of a Person with
> Leprosy

Take a few minutes to savour a word, a phrase, a question, or a feeling that rises up in you. Reflect on this quietly or share it aloud. (The other Scripture readings of the day are Leviticus 13:1-2, 44-46 and 1 Corinthians 10:31-11:1.)

Invitation to Reflect on the Gospel

This short and seemingly simple story is filled with food for reflection for us. Jesus could work miracles and people had come to know this about him. But he did not want to be known principally as a miracle worker since this is not why he came. This person with leprosy, however, came to Jesus believing in his power to cure, yet neither demanding nor expecting it. He knelt before Jesus and appealed to his compassion with the request, "if you *wish*, you can make me clean" (Mark 1:40, emphasis added). And Jesus, moved not out of desire to prove his power, but simply out of compassion and pity, chose to rid him of the disfiguring disease of leprosy.

Because of their disease, those with leprosy were confined to certain areas and could go no closer to Jerusalem than this town of Bethany. From its hilltop, they could see the Temple and the holy city just a few miles away but could not go there. It is significant that Jesus made his home in Bethany while in Jerusalem. We notice in the story that, in curing the man, Jesus touched him. At this moment of touching the person with leprosy, Jesus himself became ceremonially unclean and could not enter the Temple or synagogue. So great was his compassion and the importance of the lesson he was passing on to bystanders and to us.

While we ourselves may not be able to work miracles or cure, we can follow this example of compassion. We, too, can touch those who are suffering, touch them physically and touch their spirits by our compassionate care or assistance. If we but look we'll find lepers of all kinds, outcasts both within and outside our community, people who are looked down upon, people who are avoided, people who are just not included for whatever reason. How would Jesus treat them? This is what he wants us to do.

Invitation to Group Sharing

1. Have I ever felt like an outcast? What was that experience like? What did I want from others at that time?

2. Remember when you first came into the parish community. Were there groups or cliques that made it difficult to find a way of entering the community? Who or what helped me feel part of the community?

3. Who are the outcasts in the circles of my life? What is it that makes it difficult for us to reach out to the outcasts in today's world? What can we do for those who experience being outcasts?

Invitation to Act

Determine a specific action (individual or group) that flows from your sharing. This should be your primary consideration. When choosing an individual action, determine what you will do and share it with the group. When choosing a group action, determine who will take responsibility for different aspects of the action. The following are secondary suggestions:

1. In your own life, follow Jesus' example with the person in this story. Reach out and touch someone who may feel marginalised or may be suffering.

2. In your own family or community it may be difficult for some people to feel welcome. Decide what you can do to help your family or community groups be actively open and welcoming to all.

3. There may be outcasts in your nearby society. As a community, find out what opportunities there are to assist them and publicise these through your parish bulletin, Web site, or in your local newspaper. Act on your findings.

Invitation to Closing Prayer

Give thanks to God (aloud or silently) for insights gained, for desires awakened, for directions clarified, for the gift of one another's openness and sensitivity. Conclude with the following:

Leader   In Christ Jesus, the Son of God,
we have learned what you want of us in this life.

All   We turn to you, loving God,
to help us bring about the ideas and ideals
we have talked about together during this time.

Nothing is impossible with your help.
It is that help we ask for now
and we ask with humble hearts.
But we also ask with confidence because our faith
tells us you are there to help us do your will.

We ask these things through Christ our Lord.
Amen

Seventh Sunday in Ordinary Time

Faith in Forgiveness

Invitation to Pray

Pause for a few moments of silence and enter more deeply into the presence of God.

> ***Song:*** "Lay Your Hands," Carey Landry, North American Liturgy Resources
>
> ***Proclaim the gospel:*** Mark 2:1-12
> Healing of a Paralytic

Take a few minutes to savour a word, a phrase, a question, or a feeling that rises up in you. Reflect on this quietly or share it aloud. (The other Scripture readings of the day are Isaiah 43:18-19, 21-22, 24b-25 and 2 Corinthians 1:18-22.)

Invitation to Reflect on the Gospel

Over and over in the stories of miraculous cures, we see Jesus emphasise the importance of faith. Faith is the requirement. What faith the paralytic and his friends show! They even remove the thatched roof to get close to Jesus in the crowd. But notice what Jesus first says to the man. Before anything, Jesus forgives his sins. And he forgives him readily because the man shows that he has faith. That is, he believes in Jesus and in his power. Faith was the requirement then. It is the requirement now – that we believe, that we have faith our sins can and will be forgiven.

Forgiveness is one of the most complicated human experiences. Sometimes, just asking for forgiveness seems impossibly hard. For some people, forgiving oneself is the stumbling block. For others, it is believing that God truly has forgiven them. And forgiving others when we feel wronged seems to be the challenge for many. Yet forgiving and being forgiven are basic to our faith. The need to forgive and be forgiven never leaves us throughout our life. As long as we interact with other human beings it is there.

What is the role of faith in this? Our faith tells us that forgiveness is essential. Faith gives us the courage and strength to take whatever steps we need to take. It reminds us that this is what Jesus asks and demands of his followers. Faith showers us with God's love, which enables us to know that we are loved and forgiven and that we can follow the example of Christ to forgive.

Invitation to Group Sharing

1. When did someone forgive me when I needed it? What was that experience like?

2. The reflection mentions several difficulties people have with forgiveness. What is the hardest part for me?

3. What role do you see forgiveness playing in your personal life at home, with your friends, and/or in the workplace?

4. What messages does our culture give about forgiving and being forgiven? How can we consistently share the value of forgiveness?

Invitation to Act

Determine a specific action (individual or group) that flows from your sharing. This should be your primary consideration. When choosing an individual action, determine what you will do and share it with the group. When choosing a group action, determine who will take responsibility for different aspects of the action. The following are secondary suggestions:

1. At the end of each day this week, think back over the times when the need for forgiveness was there in yourself or those around you. Pray for the insight to recognise those times as soon as they occur.

2. Choose one way to be a forgiving person this week. Forgive yourself, ask forgiveness of another, or offer it to someone who is seeking it from you. Pray in thanksgiving for that grace.

3. Celebrate the Sacrament of Reconciliation.

4. Decide as a group from whom you need to ask forgiveness for social sins of prejudice or neglect. Together, write a note or visit in person a group whom you are in need of asking forgiveness for past injuries.

Invitation to Closing Prayer

Give thanks to God (aloud or silently) for insights gained, for desires awakened, for directions clarified, for the gift of one another's openness and sensitivity. Conclude with the following:

Leader   We pray together the Lord's Prayer
every time we celebrate the Eucharist.
We ask God to give us the courage to pray
this prayer with meaning now
for it is a prayer that asks forgiveness
and that challenges us to forgive as Jesus taught.
Together let us pray this prayer slowly.

All   Our Father...

Eighth Sunday in Ordinary Time

New Covenant of Love

Invitation to Pray

Pause for a few moments of silence and enter more deeply into the presence of God.

> *Song:* "Love is His Word," Luke Connaughton, McCrimon Publishing Co Ltd
>
> *Proclaim the gospel:* Mark 2:18-22
> The Bridegroom Is Still with Them

Take a few minutes to savour a word, a phrase, a question, or a feeling that rises up in you. Reflect on this quietly or share it aloud. (The other Scripture readings of the day are Hosea 2:16b, 17b, 21-22 and 2 Corinthians 3:1b-6.)

Invitation to Reflect on the Gospel

Coming as it often does just before Lent, this gospel may seem to contradict the Lenten call to fasting that will soon echo throughout the Church. If we stand back and take a look at the whole liturgical year, though, we realise that we are called to both fasting and feasting at different times in the year. Both are part of the Christian life. We simply focus on different aspects at different times. In Lent, we are called to follow the example of Jesus' forty days in the desert, fasting and other-wise emptying ourselves so we can confront the reality of that which needs to be forgiven and reconciled in our lives. At other times, such as the Easter season and today, the readings remind us that Christ is alive and the kingdom of God is a present reality, and that is cause for festive celebration.
The image of the bridegroom in the gospel relates back to the

marriage imagery in the first reading for this Sunday. Hosea's fidelity to an unfaithful spouse illustrates the covenant between the faithful God and the occasionally wayward Israel. The gospel points to a new covenant that God has established in Jesus: a covenant of love that transcends the practice of fasting and, at the same time, calls for a new way of living. Here, Jesus is the bridegroom whose presence is reason to refrain from fasting. Jesus does not reject fasting; in fact, he anticipates that day "when the bridegroom is taken away from them, and then they will fast" (Mark 2:20). Rather, he uses the image of the cloth and the wineskins to suggest that this new covenant requires a new way of life that must be visible in those who undertake external practices such as fasting. This is not unlike what we will hear on Ash Wednesday when, in the first reading, God sets fasting within the larger call to "return to me with your whole heart" and exhorts us to "rend your hearts, not your garments" (Joel 2:12-13).

God's new covenant of love has taken flesh in Jesus. May we who profess to be his followers be the new wineskins that bear the new wine of this covenant to a thirsting world.

Invitation to Group Sharing

1. How might I describe the covenant God has established with those who are baptised, including myself?

2. What does this new covenant of love require of me? How am I living out the responsibilities of this covenant?

3. What are the areas of my life that need to be renewed so that I might bear God's new covenant of love to others?

Invitation to Act

Determine a specific action (individual or group) that flows from your sharing. This should be your primary consideration. When choosing an individual action, determine what you will do and share it with the group. When choosing a group action, determine who will take responsibility for different aspects of the action. The following are secondary suggestions:

1. Reflect on the times in your life when you discovered a new insight into your faith or when you had a renewed experience of your faith. Think about who or what made that possible, and thank God for them. Pray for the ability to be open to new growth in your faith today and in the future.

2. Those who are poor often have to choose involuntarily between fasting from food and fasting from other life essentials, such as new clothes, heat during winter, or secure shelter. Find out about organisations that make life necessities more accessible to those who are poor, and make this information available through the parish office and local social service agencies. Act on this information.

3. Fast from prejudice and injustice against others. Share ways you can do this through your small community. Act on your suggestions.

Invitation to Closing Prayer

Give thanks to God (aloud or silently) for insights gained, for desires awakened, for directions clarified, for the gift of one another's openness and sensitivity. Conclude with the following:

Leader Faithful God, in baptism you made us partners
      in the new covenant of love
      that you established in Jesus, your Son.

      Strengthen us to turn away from old ways of sin,
      open us to the newness of life you offer,
      and renew our commitment to share your mission
      and to serve others.
      We ask this through the same Christ our Lord.

All   Amen

Ninth Sunday in Ordinary Time

Master of the Sabbath

Invitation to Pray

Pause for a few moments of silence and enter more deeply into presence of God.

> ***Song:*** "Sing to the Mountains," Robert J. Dufford, SJ, OCP

> ***Proclaim the gospel:*** Mark 2:23-3:6
> The Son of Man Is Lord Even of the Sabbath

Take a few minutes to savour a word, a phrase, a question, or a feeling that rises up in you. Reflect on this quietly or share it aloud. (The other Scripture readings of the day are Deuteronomy 5:12-15 and 2 Corinthians 4:6-11.)

Invitation to Reflect on the Gospel

On the surface, this gospel may appear to be a simple case in which Jesus is attacking an outdated piece of religious legislation that clearly made no sense. Those who are naturally distrustful of laws may find this scenario quite appealing! When seen against the background provided in the first reading, though, the gospel story begins to reveal a much deeper message. In the first reading from Deuteronomy, we discover that the law of Sabbath rest is intrinsically tied to Jewish identity. The prohibition from work on the seventh day was a symbol of the freedom the Jewish people enjoyed, in contrast to the enslavement they experienced in Egypt. It is an affirmation they are the people whom God had chosen and liberated from slavery.

161

To some of the Pharisees, Jesus caused an affront to his Jewish faith when he allowed his disciples to pick the ears of corn on the Sabbath. On one level, the Pharisees were right: in their interpretation, thirty-nine types of work were forbidden on the Sabbath. In response, Jesus appeals to a deeper value. He recalls the precedent of David, who fed his hungry companions from food that was reserved for the priests (1 Samuel 21:2-7), and then declares that, "the sabbath was made for man, not man for the sabbath" (Mark 2:27). Moving into the synagogue, he cures the man with a withered hand, thus expanding the provision in Jewish law that one could save a life on the Sabbath, to include doing good in a situation that was not life threatening. Jesus' purpose is not to dismiss the law concerning Sabbath rest, but rather to point out that even this important commandment must yield to other more fundamental commandments. In determining which commandments are greater than the observance of Sabbath rest, Jesus establishes himself as "master of the Sabbath."

Today's gospel is not an invitation to casually disregard the law, whether it is the law of state, nation, or Church. It is a reminder that the most fundamental commandments are those that call us to feed the hungry, to heal the sick, and to love one another. These are the primary laws that should form our identity as those who follow the "master of the Sabbath."

Invitation to Group Sharing

1. How do I understand Jesus' statement that "the sabbath was made for man, not man for the sabbath" (Mark 2:27)?

2. Am I content to observe the "letter of the law" while not attending to its deepest meaning? Does my attitude toward law allow for the kind of love and charity that Jesus practiced in spite of its apparent prohibition?

3. How do we observe the Lord's Day in our households and in our local communities?

4. How do we create and/or protect times of rest from work in our contemporary lives? Are there ways we could do this better?

Invitation to Act

Determine a specific action (individual or group) that flows from your sharing. This should be your primary consideration. When choosing an individual action, determine what you will do and share it with the group. When choosing a group action, determine who will take responsibility for different aspects of the action. The following are secondary suggestions:

1. If you serve in a parish ministry, become familiar with Church documents that pertain to this ministry.

2. Read or prayerfully reflect on the biblical account of the Ten Commandments (Exodus 20:1-17), Jesus' response to the question "Which is the first of all the commandments?" (Mark 12:28-34), and Jesus' declaration of the new commandment (John 13:34-35; 15:12-17). Journal your reflections and from time to time go back to pray through these again.

3. Invite family or friends over for an "old fashioned Sunday dinner" after Mass this Sunday or next. Try to keep Sunday as free from work as possible. If you have a job that requires you to work on Sunday, make time some other day during the week to rest from your labours.

4. Read the papal encyclical 'On keeping the Sabbath

Day Holy'. It is available from good Catholic bookshops or can be found at www.vatican.va/holy_father/john_paul_ii/apost_ letters/documents/hf_jp-ii_apl_05071998_ dies-domini_en.html

Invitation to Closing Prayer

Give thanks to God (aloud or silently) for insights gained, for desires awakened, for directions clarified, for the gift of one another's openness and sensitivity. Conclude with the following:

Leader   God of all times, you give us days to work
and days to rest from our labours.
Help us to follow your Son,
the master of the Sabbath,
who taught us to see in each day
the opportunity to serve one another in charity.
We ask this through the same Christ our Lord.

All   Amen

Tenth Sunday in Ordinary Time

Collaborative Ministry

Invitation to Pray

Pause for a few moments of silence and enter more deeply into the presence of God.

> ***Song:*** "City of God," Dan Schutte, OCP

> ***Proclaim the gospel:*** Mark 3:20-35
> Doing God's Will Together

Take a few minutes to savour a word, a phrase, a question, or a feeling that rises up in you. Reflect on this quietly or share it aloud. (The other Scripture readings of the day are Genesis 3:9-15 and 2 Corinthians 4:13-5:1.)

Invitation to Reflect on the Gospel

"Who are my mother and [my] brothers?" (Mark 3:33). It's hardly the kind of response that warms the heart of a mother who has come out to greet a returning son. Little wonder that Jesus' relatives were afraid he was out of his mind! Jesus' homecoming causes as much of an uproar as the scenes we heard in the gospels of the two previous Sundays in Ordinary Time. Once again, Jesus says something that is outrageous on the surface to force his listeners to consider its deeper meaning.

There is no evidence that Jesus had anything but the deepest love and respect for his mother. His question "Who are my mother and [my] brothers?" (Mark 3:33) is not a rejection of his earthly family, but rather a declaration that all who do the will of God are part of his family. By using the image of a family, Jesus provides an insight into the kind of relationship he expects among his followers. They are not to be like a kingdom or a house divided against itself, rather they are to carry out their mission as brothers and sisters. To use contemporary jargon, Jesus calls his followers to a collaborative ministry. In collaborative ministry, as in a healthy family, the unique, God-given gifts and talents of each person are respected and unselfishly put to the service of the whole. As Saint Paul said, "To each individual the manifestation of the Spirit is given for some benefit" (1 Corinthians 12:7).

The face of ministry in our Church continues to evolve. Priests may not oversee numerous assistant priests as in the past, but especially in large parishes they do lead increasingly large and diverse staffs made up of deacons, religious sisters and brothers, and lay people, perhaps including pastoral ministers trained in religious education, liturgy, music, and youth ministry, business administrators and a variety of support personnel. Staff members, in turn, work with a variety of volunteer ministers. The growth of these various ministries has often been called a sign of the Spirit's work in the contemporary Church. When the ministers of a parish work collaboratively, the parish is usually full of life. When they don't, the parish may be like the kingdom or the house divided against itself, which, Jesus says, "will not be able to stand" (Mark 3:25). May our parishes be among those that stand and thrive!

Invitation to Group Sharing

1. In what ways am I doing the will of God at this point in my life?

2. Are there people doing the will of God whom I am unwilling to accept as brothers and sisters of Jesus? If so, how can I change my will to love and accept them?

3. What are the things that are fostering and nurturing collaborative ministry in our parish? What are the things that are blocking or inhibiting collaborative ministry in our parish?

4. How can we, individually or as a group, help foster and nurture collaborative ministry in our parish?

Invitation to Act

Determine a specific action (individual or group) that flows from your sharing. This should be your primary consideration. When choosing an individual action, determine what you will do and share it with the group. When choosing a group action, determine who will take responsibility for different aspects of the action. The following are secondary suggestions:

1. Think about the people with whom you minister. Think about the gifts and talents each of them brings to the parish. Thank God for them. Thank them for the unique contribution they make to the life of the parish.

2. The Diocese of Westminster has undertaken to develop collaborative ministry. Go to the 'Graced by the Spirit' website (www.gracedbythespirit.org.uk) to discover both the theology and the practical implications at the heart of this development.

3. Take the time to find out what led others in your group to their ministry and what nourishes them spiritually. Put time and energy into spiritual development with your fellow ministers. Start meetings with prayer. (Encourage the use of *PRAYERTIME Cycles A, B, C* for all ministries). Consider an annual retreat or seasonal days of reflection for the group.

Invitation to Closing Prayer

Give thanks to God (aloud or silently) for insights gained, for desires awakened, for directions clarified, for the gift of one another's openness and sensitivity. Conclude with the following:

Leader   Lord God and Father of us all,
you sent Jesus into our midst
to gather in one family all who do your will.
May all we do in your name
form us into a strong household,
united in its service of your reign.
We ask this through Christ our Lord.

All   Amen

Eleventh Sunday in Ordinary Time

Seeds of Hope

Invitation to Pray

Pause for a few moments of silence and enter more deeply into the presence of God.

> *Song:* "The Kingdom of God is Justice and Joy,"
> Bryn Rees

> *Proclaim the gospel:* Mark 4:26-34
> The Mustard Seed

Take a few minutes to savour a word, a phrase, a question, or a feeling that rises up in you. Reflect on this quietly or share it aloud. (The other Scripture readings of the day are Ezekiel 17:22-24 and 2 Corinthians 5:6-10.)

Invitation to Reflect on the Gospel

One of the first science experiments nursery school children do is to plant some seeds in a milk carton, which is then left by the classroom window to be warmed by the sun. There is always a great deal of excitement when the first plant sprouts: after watering and watching for any number of days and seeing nothing, finally there is the first sign of life. Something much bigger is growing from something much smaller, all because they put a little seed in some soil with their own hands.

What a sense of hope these images of the growing seed and the mustard seed must have given to Jesus' followers and Mark's readers. The first believers suffered tremendously for their faith, and to understand that the kingdom of God starts as something no bigger than a seed, which then grows into something large and sturdy, must have been a real encouragement. They were at the very beginning of something they could scarcely imagine would have the effect on the world it has had. These parables abound with the themes of strength, patience, persistence, fortitude…and hope.

In a world and a society that are often darkened by storm clouds of war, greed, injustice, poverty, racism, religious persecution, political manipulation, and self-centredness, we need to hear this gospel as much as Mark's readers did. The growth of a seed is imperceptible; it happens over time, and we cannot make it grow. All we can do is work to provide the right environment and trust that by doing our part, the seed will do what it is meant to do: grow. Trees have been known to split rocks and concrete as they grow, and even the tiniest weeds find a way to spring up through asphalt. Just as the early Church could not know the effect its faith would have on the world, we cannot know how *our* faith will effect the furthering of the reign of God for those who come after us. Our job is to cultivate the soil of our lives and live the Word of God. Though perhaps imperceptibly at first, that Word will do what it is meant to do if we are but open and fertile.

Invitation to Group Sharing

1. Whom do I know who seems to live a life of gospel hope in spite of challenging circumstances? What is it that makes him or her so?

2. What are the ways in which I keep the soil of my life cultivated so that it's a healthy growing medium for the Word of God? Are there things I could do differently?

3. What do I do to participate in or witness to the reign of God? Reflect broadly! This is not limited only to what would be considered "religious acts."

4. How are we, as individuals and as a parish, branches of that tree in which "the birds of the sky can dwell in [our] shade" (Mark 4:32)? What can we do to be so?

Invitation to Act

Determine a specific action (individual or group) that flows from your sharing. This should be your primary consideration. When choosing an individual action, determine what you will do and share it with the group. When choosing a group action, determine who will take responsibility for different aspects of the action. The following are secondary suggestions:

1. As a spiritual exercise, get a small pot (or milk carton!), some soil and plant something – flower, vegetable, herb, it doesn't really matter. Do this even if you already have a garden, and let this little pot be a focus for your prayer and reflection. If it gets too large for its container, transplant it outside. From sowing to flower or harvest, keep a little notebook to track its progress. Use your journal if you have one. Try to be aware of ways in which your faith and relationship with God are similar to the growing of the seed.

2. Consider participating in the *RCIA* in your parish as either a catechist or sponsor. If your parish does not have that particular framework for adult initiation, speak to your priest or someone on the pastoral team to see what is provided.

3. Discover what provision there is for adult faith formation in your parish. Commit yourself to help developing this programme.

4. Explore the possibility of organizing a community garden with some of the other churches in your area. The produce grown can be distributed to parishioners in need, or your local soup kitchen. Flowers can be grown and given to the housebound.

Invitation to Closing Prayer

Give thanks to God (aloud or silently) for insights gained, for desires awakened, for directions clarified, for the gift of one another's openness and sensitivity. Conclude with the following:

Gracious God,
you provide for us always.
These early summer days explode
with the glory of greening and growing;
small seeds putting forth shoots,
and trees expanding their reach
as their canopies flourish and fill.

May they always be for us physical reminders
of the presence of your kingdom.

May our hope be as constant as the leaves
that grow back year after year.

And may that hope be a haven
for those who need rest.

With praise for the glory of these days
we offer our prayer in Jesus' name. Amen

Twelfth Sunday in Ordinary Time

Presence during the Storm

Invitation to Pray

Pause for a few moments of silence and enter more deeply into the presence of God.

> *Song:* "O Changeless Christ," vv1-3,
> Timothy Dudley-Smith

> *Proclaim the gospel:* Mark 4:35-41
> Calming the Storm at Sea

Take a few minutes to savour a word, a phrase, a question, or a feeling that rises up in you. Reflect on this quietly or share it aloud. (The other Scripture readings of the day are Job 38:1, 8-11 and 2 Corinthians 5:14-17.)

Invitation to Reflect on the Gospel

Many of us have had the experience of either driving or being a passenger in a vehicle when without warning, the skies open up and we're in the middle of a downpour or blinding snow storm. The visibility decreases dramatically, road conditions are unsafe, and we're not sure if we should pull off the road. It can be very alarming, not unlike what the disciples experienced in the boat with Jesus.

This story is not only about Jesus' power over the wind and sea; it is about Jesus' presence *during* the storm. Trust is a quality that is built over time and through experience. When we are feeling overwhelmed by upsetting circumstances, it is easy to think God has broken trust with us. When a storm is swirling about us, it is easy to lose our sense of direction and become confused as to what the next step ought to be. The practices of prayer, reading, and quiet time can get lost in the confusion, and when we seemingly lose that connection with God, maintaining trust becomes even harder.

A powerful aspect of the Jewish Passover celebration, which we experience most fully during the Easter Vigil, is the retelling of the stories of God's deliverance of the Hebrew people. The stories - of their release by Pharaoh, the parting of the sea, the cloud by day and pillar of fire by night - are told year after year so they are always reminded that God heard their cry, set them free, and *travelled with them* to the Promised Land. By recalling what God has done for *us*, we remember God's unwavering presence in our lives and reinforce the sometimes thin thread of trust when rough seas buffet us. We are reminded that even during the most distressing times, we are *never* alone. And after the storms have passed, we may find we have the grace to answer this most profound question, "Who then is this that even wind and sea obey him?" (Mark 4:41).

Invitation to Group Sharing

1. Have I ever felt that Jesus was "asleep in the boat"? What did I do?

2. What do I do in my relationship with God to keep the trust strong?

3. How could we, as a group or parish, work together to build trust amongst ourselves so that our commitment to God, one another, and the larger community is strengthened?

Invitation to Act

Determine a specific action (individual or group) that flows from your sharing. This should be your primary consideration. When choosing an individual action, determine what you will do and share it with the group. When choosing a group action, determine who will take responsibility for different aspects of the action. The following are secondary suggestions:

1. If you do not already do this, establish a habit of prayer or quiet time on a regular basis.

2. Take time to chronicle some events in your life when you have been tossed about by distressing circumstances. Consider the ways God was present to you. Write all this down so the next time the seas get rocky, you will have your own stories of God's faithfulness from which to draw upon.

3. Try to be the calming presence to someone you know who may be experiencing some turbulence in his or her life right now.

Invitation to Closing Prayer

Give thanks to God (aloud or silently) for insights gained, for desires awakened, for directions clarified, for the gift of one another's openness and sensitivity. Conclude with the following:

Creator of the wind and sea,
storms and distractions abound
as we move through our daily lives.

When all around us is crashing and shifting,
we often lose our ability
to keep our eyes and hearts trained on you.

We forget who you are
and our faith becomes fragile.

During these times, bring to mind
the many ways you have been present to us in the past,
and help us to experience your presence.

Forgive us when we doubt you,
and deepen our ability to trust.

We offer this prayer through Christ our Lord.

Amen

Thirteenth Sunday in Ordinary Time

Ministering Faith

Invitation to Pray

Pause for a few moments of silence and enter more deeply into the presence of God.

> ***Song:*** "O Changeless Christ," vv1-2, 4-5, Timothy Dudley-Smith

> ***Proclaim the gospel:*** Mark 5:21-43
> Jairus' Daughter and the Woman with a Hemorrhage

Take a few minutes to savour a word, a phrase, a question, or a feeling that rises up in you. Reflect on this quietly or share it aloud. (The other Scripture readings of the day are Wisdom 1:13-15; 2:23-24 and 2 Corinthians 8:7, 9, 13-15.)

Invitation to Reflect on the Gospel

What wonderfully powerful events are proclaimed in this gospel! We hear of humility, faith, and power over sickness and death; we hear of salvation. We hear that Jesus' compassion encompasses a man in public leadership as well as a woman who is not even named. Both Jairus and the woman fell at Jesus' feet: one at the asking and the other upon realising that she had received healing. They both believed that simply by Jesus' touch and the slightest contact with his clothing, they would be relieved of their misery. The woman, because of her flow of blood, would be considered unclean by Jewish law. And if Jairus' daughter were truly dead, Jesus would become unclean by touching her. A person who touches one who is unclean is then considered unclean also, but the compassion of Jesus transcends this situation.

In both these stories, people in crisis are moving toward Jesus, almost being propelled from a place of desperation to a place of faith. In their meeting Jesus, he treats them both with the same generosity and sensitivity. He does not push the woman aside because he is preoccupied with the needs of a synagogue official. He holds up the whole procession to address her tenderly. Both here and at Jairus' house, Jesus ignores the sentiments of the crowds, sentiments of incredulity and ridicule. What matters to Jesus is the faith with which he has been approached. In both instances it is faith that leads to salvation: to the woman he says, "Daughter, your faith has saved you" (Mark 5:34), and to Jairus, "Do not be afraid; just have faith" (Mark 5:36).

This gospel gives a very clear picture of how we, individually and as a community, are called to minister. When we minister in Jesus' name there is no place for preferential treatment; compassion and single-minded attentiveness are essential. We are also given moving examples of how to approach Jesus with the needs of our hearts: with humility and sincerity of faith. It is only with humility and faith that we can truly minister with equality, compassion, and clarity.

Invitation to Group Sharing

1. Have there been circumstances in my life when I have been like Jairus or the woman with the haemorrhage? When have I been like the apostles in the crowd or the mourners at Jairus' house?

2. Has there ever been a time when I found myself avoiding a certain ministry because it might bring me into contact with people who may be a little less desirable to be around? What was it? What did I do?

3. Jairus' faith saved his daughter; what impact can my faith have on those around me? How will I extend my compassion to that person or those persons?

4. Who are the 'unclean' in my neighbourhood or place of work that need my compassion?

Invitation to Act

Determine a specific action (individual or group) that flows from your sharing. This should be your primary consideration. When choosing an individual action, determine what you will do and share it with the group. When choosing a group action, determine who will take responsibility for different aspects of the action. The following are secondary suggestions:

1. During your prayer time, let yourself fall at Jesus' feet as you bring him someone or something in your life in need of healing. What does he say to you?

2. If you are a extraordinary minister of communion, try to see the people who come to you for the Body and Blood of Jesus as either Jairus or the woman with the haemorrhage, in need of Jesus' healing touch.

3. Use the Internet to read about Saint Damien de Veuster, Belgian missionary to leprosy patients on the Hawaiian island of Molokai. Share what you learn with someone this week.

4. Contact your Diocesan Offices and find out how your parish can become involved with the local ministries to those in need.

Invitation to Closing Prayer

Give thanks to God (aloud or silently) for insights gained, for desires awakened, for directions clarified, for the gift of one another's openness and sensitivity. Conclude with the following:

> God, ever near to us,
> your tenderness toward us
> is so clear as we hear Jesus assure Jairus,
> and address the nameless woman as "daughter."
>
> May they inspire us to approach you
> with such bold humility and faith.
>
> Enlarge our hearts that in our ministry
> we would imitate Jesus in his compassion
> for people in all stations of society.
>
> Break down the barriers of fear
> that keep us from serving those
> who are considered "unclean."
>
> And keep us focused on the work
> you set before us, that by our touch,
> your touch will be felt.
>
> In Jesus' name we offer you
> our hands and hearts. Amen

Fourteenth Sunday in Ordinary Time

Faith and Rejection

Invitation to Pray

Pause for a few moments of silence and enter more deeply into the presence of God.

> ***Song:*** "I Heard the Voice of Jesus Say,"
> Horatius Bonar

> ***Proclaim the gospel:*** Mark 6:1-6
> Rejection at Nazareth

Take a few minutes to savour a word, a phrase, a question, or a feeling that rises up in you. Reflect on this quietly or share it aloud. (The other Scripture readings of the day are Ezekiel 2:2-5 and 2 Corinthians 12:7-10.)

Invitation to Reflect on the Gospel

Being rejected, questioned, and doubted were not new or foreign experiences to Jesus. Since the beginning of his public ministry, he was an open target to the religious leaders of his day. What we hear in this gospel, though, is that those with whom Jesus lived and grew rejected him. Their questions: "Where did this man get all this? What kind of wisdom... What mighty deeds..." (Mark 6:2) seem to echo more cynicism and suspicion than awe.

The pain of rejection is something most of us experience at one time or another. Whether we are rejected for things we say or do, for how we believe and live, or even for how we dress and with whom we associate, the pain of being misunderstood and not accepted can run very deep. After people have an experience that brings them to explore their faith on a whole new level, they may find themselves being chided or teased by those with whom they are most familiar. Those whom they have known for many years know the old patterns, habits, and flaws and are quick to point them out as those first few "baby steps" of faith are taken. They may feel threatened by the changes they see and their reaction may be one of rejection.

Jesus' very human response to the crowd's rejection is one of amazement. He is bringing to his "native place" (Mark 6:1) the good news of salvation, yet the people will not hear it and so his ability to work the same kind of miracles as he did for Jairus' daughter and the woman with the haemorrhage is dramatically diminished. Yet that did not stop him from doing what he was able to do or from carrying on with the work to which he was called. When how we live changes because of a faith or conversion experience, it is helpful to remember that we are not alone when we face rejection and misunderstanding from the people to whom we are closest. Jesus gives us the very grace he possessed so that we may carry on and be faithful to the work at hand.

Invitation to Group Sharing

1. In what ways have I experienced rejection or misunderstanding? Without naming aloud specific people, who was the source and what was the reason? How did I feel then? How do I feel about that person now?

2. When and why have I rejected others?

3. Have I ever allowed myself to be caught up in a "group reaction" to someone? If this ever happens again, how can I be prepared to respond in truth and love?

4. How am I to act when I experience rejection?

Invitation to Act

Determine a specific action (individual or group) that flows from your sharing. This should be your primary consideration. When choosing an individual action, determine what you will do and share it with the group. When choosing a group action, determine who will take responsibility for different aspects of the action. The following are secondary suggestions:

1. In prayer, recall times of rejection that may still be difficult for you to accept. Bring the people and situations involved into your prayer and ask God for the grace to forgive if there is still a need for forgiveness.

2. Make an honest examination of the times you have rejected others and consider bringing that to the sacrament of reconciliation. Apologise and be reconciled.

3. As individuals or as a group, make an effort to reach out to those in your parish who seem to be on the fringes of involvement and may need some encouragement to become active members of the parish.

Invitation to Closing Prayer

Give thanks to God (aloud or silently) for insights gained, for desires awakened, for directions clarified, for the gift of one another's openness and sensitivity. Conclude with the following:

God of mercy,
at one time or another
we have all been on both sides
of rejection and misunderstanding.

Where we need to forgive,
please give us the grace to do so.

Where we need to seek forgiveness,
please give us the courage to seek it.

With single-minded commitment,
help us to do the work
to which we are called,
even as we face challenging situations.

Help us to be open to the prophets
in our own midst,
so we do not fail to hear your voice
in the ones with whom we live, work, and worship.

We make our prayer through Christ our Lord. Amen

Fifteenth Sunday in Ordinary Time

Called to Discipleship

Invitation to Pray

Pause for a few moments of silence and enter more deeply into the presence of God.

> *Song:* "Go to the World,"
> Sylvia Dunstan, GIA

> *Proclaim the gospel:* Mark 6:7-13
> Mission of the Twelve

Take a few minutes to savour a word, a phrase, a question, or a feeling that rises up in you. Reflect on this quietly or share it aloud. (The other Scripture readings of the day are Amos 7:12-15 and Ephesians 1:3-14.)

Invitation to Reflect on the Gospel

The first sentence in this gospel is enough to take your breath away: "He summoned the Twelve and began to send them out…and gave them authority…" (Mark 6:7). The disciples had been with Jesus for a while. They had heard him preach; they had seen him perform miracles. They had also seen him be rejected. Now it was their turn to go out and do what they had seen him do. Even though this was the first time, Jesus' instructions are minimal and austere. The bottom line seems to be, "Go, do what I have done, be aware that you will face difficulty, and trust that your needs will be met."

Imagine Jesus standing before you, your prayer group, or committee and saying those words to you. That is exactly what happens when we are dismissed, or rather sent forth, from our eucharistic celebrations every Sunday. The time and place, the culture and circumstances are different, but the call is the same. The mission Jesus gave to his disciples and gives to us is not something that originates within himself; it is the mission that comes from the Father manifested at his baptism by John. When we were baptised, we were anointed "priest, prophet, and king." By our baptism, we are summoned and given the challenge to be bearers of the Good News and to preach repentance.

Twenty-first century western civilisation is a far cry from first century Palestine. Simplifying our 'load' presents more of a challenge than it did two thousand years ago, but it is not impossible. We may not be travelling to nearby towns or distant shores in missionary work; perhaps our own mission field is our family, our workplace, our school, our neighbourhood, or even our own parish. We have the opportunity to respond to the summons, to our baptismal call, on a daily basis.

Invitation to Group Sharing

1. Have I ever had the sense of being 'called' to do something? (It doesn't have to be big!) How did I know? What were the circumstances? How did I respond?

2. Why might Jesus have been so specific about what the disciples were to bring and not bring on their journey? How do I apply this teaching (or instruction) to my own life?

3. In what ways am I aware of the mission given to *me* by Jesus, by virtue of my baptism? Do I trust that commission? What does it mean to me?

4. What has been my experience when I have shared my faith and relationship with Jesus with someone? Have I been welcomed, disregarded, or somewhere in between the two? What will I do to share my faith with someone this week?

Invitation to Act

Determine a specific action (individual or group) that flows from your sharing. This should be your primary consideration. When choosing an individual action, determine what you will do and share it with the group. When choosing a group action, determine who will take responsibility for different aspects of the action. The following are secondary suggestions:

1. Ask a member of your parish staff if you could borrow a book that contains the Rite of Baptism. Slowly read the prayers and explanations of the Rite, and think about how these words and instances of anointing have affected your life. *Think about who you are as a baptised person.* As well as individually, consider doing this in your group or committee setting.

2. Make a list of the 'trappings' (the "second tunic" [Mark 6:9]) that may be encumbrances in your witness to the Good News of Jesus in your life. Decide what to do with them.

3. Consider establishing an annual, parish-wide 'Commissioning Sunday.' This is not just for those actively involved in ministries; emphasise that being 'called and sent' is the privilege and responsibility of *every* baptised person.

4. Resolve to reach out effectively to members of your immediate and extended family.

5. Think creatively how evangelisation and social action go hand-in-hand. Organise groups of people, in addition to already existing committees, that will take responsibility for ministering to the needs of the wider community: a local free health clinic, childcare assistance, an affordable housing coalition, AIDS action group, hospice agencies, etc.

Invitation to Closing Prayer

Give thanks to God (aloud or silently) for insights gained, for desires awakened, for directions clarified, for the gift of one another's openness and sensitivity. Conclude with the following:

Gracious God,

in Jesus' words today
we are invited to be partners
in his work of witnessing to your kingdom on earth.

In his words,
we are reminded of the mission and responsibility
that we received in our baptism.

Keep our hearts, eyes, and ears open,
so that daily we will respond to your call.

With courage and humility, relying on your grace,
may we be agents of healing,
bearers of truth,
and messengers of hope.

We offer this prayer through Jesus Christ our Lord. Amen

Sixteenth Sunday in Ordinary Time

Rest and Renewal

Invitation to Pray

Pause for a few moments of silence and enter more deeply into the presence of God.

> *Song:* "Here I Am, Lord," Dan Schutte, OCP

> *Proclaim the gospel:* Mark 6:30-34
> Return of the Twelve

Take a few minutes to savour a word, a phrase, a question, or a feeling that rises up in you. Reflect on this silently or share it aloud. (The other Scripture readings of the day are Jeremiah 23:1-6 and Ephesians 2:13-18.)

Invitation to Reflect on the Gospel

The apostles have just returned from their first "missionary journey," and they have much to report to Jesus. You can almost imagine the disciples' excitement, and the care in Jesus' voice as he invites them to "come away...to a deserted place and rest a while" (Mark 6:31). Yet when they are faced with a crowd they forgo their rest and Jesus responds to the people as a shepherd would respond to his lost sheep. In this gospel, we see Jesus setting two examples: his invitation to come away and rest, and his tender response to the crowds who have sought them out.

Ministering to God's people is rewarding and exhausting. Whether lay or ordained, volunteer or paid, full-time or part-time, actively participating in the life of the Church requires a solid spiritual foundation, commitment, and energy. To live the Paschal Mystery is to enter into the rhythm of dying and rising in our everyday life. There are a number of times when the gospels tell us that Jesus went away to a quiet place to pray and be with his Father. Perhaps it was one of these times that prepared him to meet this crowd. To live this rhythm as the reality of our life, it is important that we know the voice of the Shepherd, listen to what he has to say, and faithfully follow him. Just as Jesus knew his Father's voice, we must know Jesus' voice.

Today's gospel finds us in the middle of Ordinary Time, in the middle of the summer, a good time to pause and catch our breath. Finding the balance of knowing when to attend to our own needs and when to care for others is not easy to achieve. It sometimes seems when we are most tired physically and spiritually, that is the time when a phone call comes, a request is made, and we must draw a deep breath and respond as best as we are able. Learning to know the voice of the Good Shepherd, and looking to his example, will help us to discern when to do the good works and when to take rest.

Invitation to Group Sharing

1. How do I maintain a balance between ministering to others' needs and taking the necessary time for rest and prayer? What happens when that balance is not met?

2. The gospel tells us that the apostles "reported all they had done and taught" (Mark 6:30) when they met with Jesus. How do we, individually and as a group, discern the right time to rest and retreat and when to respond to an immediate need as it arises?

3. What is the value of having a spiritual director or someone else to meet with and talk to about how God is present and active in my life?

4. In what ways have I learned to recognise Jesus' voice? How will I be more attentive to Jesus' voice this week?

Invitation to Act

Determine a specific action (individual or group) that flows from your sharing. This should be your primary consideration. When choosing an individual action, determine what you will do and share it with the group. When choosing a group action, determine who will take responsibility for different aspects of the action. The following are secondary suggestions:

1. Determine to respond to the next person who calls in need, despite possible inconvenience.

2. Spend some time reflecting upon how you alternate being the apostles returning with news to report, being the crowd who is hungry for truth and hope, and being Jesus who extends the invitation to rest, and at the same time, responds tenderly to the many people around him.

3. After seeking advice from someone you trust, make an appointment with a spiritual director, someone with whom you can discern the ways in which you are called to minister.

4. As a group, take a retreat together facilitated by an outside person, with the only goals being prayer, refreshment of spirit, and fellowship. Plan another time for work and discernment about the ministry in which you are involved.

Invitation to Closing Prayer

Give thanks to God (aloud or silently) for insights gained, for desires awakened, for directions clarified, for the gift of one another's openness and sensitivity. Conclude with the following:

Jesus our shepherd,

sometimes the excitement of our ministry
is matched only by the fatigue
that creeps in upon us.

When we grow weary
help us to have the wisdom to stop, even if briefly,
to sit a while with you and listen to you.

In our rest, open our eyes anew
to the many around us who need a touch,
a word, or a companion,
and grant us the grace to respond
with generous compassion
as we have seen you do. Amen

Seventeenth Sunday in Ordinary Time

Bread of Life

Invitation to Pray

Pause for a few moments of silence and enter more deeply into the presence of God.

> ***Song:*** "I Am the Bread of Life,"
> Suzanne Toolan, GIA

> ***Proclaim the gospel:*** John 6:1-15
> Multiplication of the Loaves

Take a few minutes to savour a word, a phrase, a question, or a feeling that rises up in you. Reflect on this quietly or share it aloud. (The other Scripture readings of the day are 2 Kings 4:42-44 and Ephesians 4:1-6.)

Invitation to Reflect on the Gospel

This portion of the gospel on the feeding of the multitude is one that is very familiar to us, and it is full of imagery pointing to Jesus being the Bread of Life. A crowd has followed Jesus because of the miracles they see him work, and it is late in the day. There are thousands to feed, not enough money, and seemingly inadequate provisions. But we know what happens when Jesus offers thanks for the meagre food at hand. There is more than enough for everyone to be filled with some left over, and all are astonished.

However, it would seem that there is more to the story than giving thanks and providing food. As the scene is opening and the situation becomes clear, Jesus poses the problem to Philip and the disciples: "Where can we buy enough food for them to eat?" (John 6:5). Yet the Scriptures tell us that Jesus already knew what he was going to do: "He said this to test him, because he himself knew what he was going to do" (John 6:6). The 'story within the story' is that Jesus uses this circumstance to bring his disciples deeper into his mission. He is encouraging them to see that his work is also *their* work. And perhaps even more subtly, Jesus is nurturing those seeds of faith, preparing them to believe things that up to this point were thought unbelievable: his suffering, death, and Resurrection.

The act of satisfying the people's physical hunger is not to be ignored. Over and over again Jesus sets the example that it is not enough to teach or preach or work miracles. Taking responsibility for those who are hungry and those less fortunate is paramount in sharing in the reign of God. When people are free from worry about having enough food and adequate shelter, the message of salvation may be more readily received. Jesus provided bread for their hunger; his life was bread for their lives. We are called to do and be the same.

Invitation to Group Sharing

1. What are some situations in which I felt overburdened, or that something seemingly impossible was being asked of me? How did I respond?

2. When have I felt, similar to Philip, that my response to a particular situation or question was being tested?

3. Who are the people who inspire me to believe the unbelievable? When I have been blessed in a particular way, what do I do with "the fragments left over" (John 6:12)?

4. How are we being challenged to participate more fully in the tangible actions required to be a true follower of

Jesus? Are we meeting those challenges? If not, what is getting in the way?

Invitation to Act

Determine a specific action (individual or group) that flows from your sharing. This should be your primary consideration. When choosing an individual action, determine what you will do and share it with the group. When choosing a group action, determine who will take responsibility for different aspects of the action. The following are secondary suggestions:

1. Spend some quiet time with this gospel, particularly Jesus' exchange with Philip and Andrew (John 6:5-10). Reflect upon and write down those times in your life when what you saw with your eyes seemed lacking but was made sufficient by God's grace, whether tangible, such as money, food, clothes, or intangible, such as happiness, peace, forgiveness.

2. Hunger takes many forms: hunger for understanding or being understood, hunger for internal peace, hunger for forgiveness, hunger for security, hunger for acceptance. Reach out to someone in your life whom you know lives with any of these hungers. Even your willing presence can make a difference.

3. Respond to Jesus' question, "Where can we buy enough food for them to eat?" (John 6:5). Contact your local food pantry to inquire about current needs. Soup kitchens and the like are often bursting at the seams during the autumn and winter, but are short on supply during the summer months, as there are no major seasons or feasts that keep those who are hungry in the forefront of our minds. Organise a parish or ecumenical community food drive.

Invitation to Closing Prayer

Give thanks to God (aloud or silently) for insights gained, for desires awakened, for directions clarified, for the gift of one another's openness and sensitivity. Conclude with the following:

Lord our God, Father of wisdom and grace,

sometimes our shortsightedness
does not allow us to see
it is the small abilities in our lives,
when offered to you with gratitude,
that can cause great things to happen.

Broaden our vision,
and increase our faith
so that we may respond confidently
and embrace more fully
the work of Jesus in our lives.

We ask this in union with the Holy Spirit
in the name of Jesus our Lord. Amen

Eighteenth Sunday in Ordinary Time

Signs of Life

Invitation to Pray

Pause for a few moments of silence and enter more deeply into the presence of God.

> *Song:* "I Am the Bread of Life," David Konstant, Kevin Mayhew Ltd
>
> *Proclaim the gospel:* John 6:24-35
> Bread of Life Discourse

Take a few minutes to savour a word, a phrase, a question, or a feeling that rises up in you. Reflect on this silently or share it aloud. (The other Scripture readings of the day are Exodus 16:2-4, 12-15 and Ephesians 4:17, 20-24.)

Invitation to Reflect on the Gospel

It is easy to see why the crowds followed Jesus: he was attentive to their physical needs and performed marvellous works. In this gospel, though, it is clear that the people 'don't get it.' They wanted another sign, more of what had just happened: they had been fed to fullness and wanted to be dazzled. Jesus' rebuke about not working for perishable food cuts straight to the heart. And the answer to their question, "What can we do to accomplish the works of God?" (John 6:28), is equally direct: "This is the work of God, that you believe in the one he sent" (John 6:29).

What are the signs for which we ask: greater job status? a bigger house? more money? None of these is intrinsically bad, but it is easy to lose sight of the fact that these aren't the most important things. Though they will not endure, there is the temptation to see them as a "sign" of God's blessing. In some sense they may well be, but they will *not* fill the hunger that goes beyond our physical need. And they can easily become distractions from what is our true work, having faith in the One sent by God.

Faith as "work" is not necessarily a new concept. However, it is something we don't think about until keeping our faith is challenged. There are many circumstances in life that present direct challenges to our faith: the illness or death of a loved one, unemployment or underemployment, a natural disaster, the killing of thousands of people as a result of racial intolerance. Just as "the good things" in life can be distracting, so it is with the difficulties and harsh realities of living in this world. During times like these, keeping faith is work.

In the exchange between Jesus and the crowd, the people are asking questions about tangible, material things. Jesus' answers call them, and us, to conversion, to see things differently. They wanted to see signs; he wanted them to see that he was the only "sign" necessary. They were still thinking about the bread that satisfied them; he wanted them to understand that he, himself, was the bread that satisfies all hunger.

Invitation to Group Sharing

1. When have I asked God for a sign? What was it and what were the circumstances?

2. Have I ever had the experience of being hungry for something without knowing exactly what it was I was hungry for? Have I raided the kitchen and 'grazed' through the cupboards until I was full, yet still didn't feel satisfied? Can I draw a parallel of this image to a time in my spiritual life?

3. Is there a person in my life who most consistently reflects "faith as work"? What is it about this person's approach to life's situations that is most inspiring?

4. How can I better respond to Jesus' call to conversion, to see beyond the bread we can hold with our hands to receiving and being the bread that is not perishable?

Invitation to Act

Determine a specific action (individual or group) that flows from your sharing. This should be your primary consideration. When choosing an individual action, determine what you will do and share it with the group. When choosing a group action, determine who will take responsibility for different aspects of the action. The following are secondary suggestions:

1. Try to get into the habit of reading the Sunday gospel before you arrive for the liturgical celebration on Saturday evening or Sunday morning. Let the bread of the Word become part of your weekly diet.

2. Whether in religious education classes, youth groups, or both, make an effort to connect the young people in your parish with the Scriptures. Catholics are not always known for their comfort level in reading the Bible and the earlier it can be introduced, the better.

3. Find out about 'World Gifts' from CAFOD. Instead of buying someone a just a gift, why not buy a goat? World Gifts is a range of gifts where everything you buy really acts as two presents in one - something for you to give a friend or relative and a real gift given to someone living in poverty.
www.cafod.org.uk/worldgifts

Invitation to Closing Prayer

Give thanks to God (aloud or silently) for insights gained, for desires awakened, for directions clarified, for the gift of one another's openness and sensitivity. Conclude with the following:

God, you who are so patient with us,

forgive us the times we have filled ourselves
with things that are perishable

and have been distracted
from doing your work
of having faith in the One you sent.

Instead of asking for signs,
help us to become signs to those in our lives
who struggle with keeping faith.

Thank you for giving us
"the food that endures for eternal life" (John 6:27)
in your Son, Jesus Christ,
through whom we are most fully satisfied
and in whose name we pray. Amen

Nineteenth Sunday in Ordinary Time

Bread from Heaven

Invitation to Pray

Pause for a few moments of silence and enter more deeply into the presence of God.

> ***Song:*** "One Bread, One Body," John Foley SJ, OCP

> ***Proclaim the gospel:*** John 6:41-51
> Bread of Life Discourse

Take a few minutes to savour a word, a phrase, a question, or a feeling that rises up in you. Reflect on this quietly or share it aloud. (The other Scripture readings of the day are 1 Kings 19:4-8 and Ephesians 4:30-5:2.)

Invitation to Reflect on the Gospel

There is no denying that Jesus is saying some hard things that are very difficult to grasp. But the people will not truly hear what Jesus says because they claim to know his family, where he grew up, how he grew up. The people of Jesus' day had been looking for a Messiah King who would change their present lot in life. Certainly God's Messiah would not come from among them, from a poor working family; he would not be a mere tradesman.

Remember last week's gospel. The people ask what it is they must do to accomplish the work of God. Jesus simply says they must "…believe in the one he sent" (John 6:29). But Jesus was not the messenger they wanted! Because their expectations were not met, their refusal to believe was strong.

Their judgment on the externals of Jesus' life prevents them from hearing and believing him when he says, "I am the bread that came down from heaven" (John 6:41). They have closed themselves off to the possibility of something greater happening in their lives.

Judging by externals is something that we do every day. Sometimes making a quick judgment is prudent. But how often have we been in situations when we have chosen to believe or disbelieve another person's words based on their appearance or what we *think* we know about them? The diminutive figure of Sister Teresa is hardly one we would imagine becoming Blessed Mother Teresa of Calcutta, one of our greatest modern-day saints. Yet her size and lack of resources did not prevent her from reaching out to the utter outcasts of society, and thereby showing us all what it is to offer life and love to others. More importantly, she showed us that the ones whom we *serve* are the living bread for us, feeding us in ways we could never imagine. God is greater than our expectations and imaginations, and will use whoever he chooses to bring about his reign here on earth.

Invitation to Group Sharing

1. Have I been in a situation in which my word was thought less of because of my appearance, perceived insufficient education, or 'social' standing? What made me aware of it? How did it feel?

2. When have I paid less attention to someone because he or she didn't look or behave in a way with which I was comfortable? Because he or she didn't fit in my circle of friends?

3. How have my expectations of a person limited my ability to recognise God's effort to reach me?

4. As a parish community, what are we doing to maintain an atmosphere of openness and receptivity toward the new ethnic groups that may be moving into our area? What can we do to become familiar with any cultural differences that may exist? What steps can we take to work toward integrating some aspects of their liturgical celebrations into the life of the parish?

Invitation to Act

Determine a specific action (individual or group) that flows from your sharing. This should be your primary consideration. When choosing an individual action, determine what you will do and share it with the group. When choosing a group action, determine who will take responsibility for different aspects of the action. The following are secondary suggestions:

1. Spend some time meditating on Jesus' words, "No one can come to me unless the Father who sent me draw him" (John 6:44). Think about what that has meant in your life. If you don't have on, this could be a good time to start a prayer journal.

2. If you are involved in any level of faith formation, from religious education of young children and teenagers to adult formation and the *RCIA*, make an effort to *really listen* to those you work with. You may be surprised to hear what God has to say to you through them. If you are not already involved, consider doing so.

3. Reach out to someone or some group in your parish, community, or family that seems to have been left out because they think or believe differently from others.

4. Contact the nearest house of the Missionaries of

Charity (Mother Teresa's community), or another group that ministers to those who are poor, and establish a relationship of service and support. The *At Your Word, Lord* Season V Action Pack / your Diocesan Pastoral Department should have suggestions.

Invitation to Closing Prayer

Give thanks to God (aloud or silently) for insights gained, for desires awakened, for directions clarified, for the gift of one another's openness and sensitivity. Conclude with the following:

Leader	In the familiar, we sometimes fail to see the holy…
All	Lord, increase our willingness and ability to see holiness in the ordinary.
Leader	In the unfamiliar, we sometimes fail to hear truth…
All	Lord, increase our willingness and ability to hear your voice in unexpected places.
Leader	In the ones we serve, we sometimes fail to embrace our own need…
All	Lord, increase our understanding that we all hunger for the Living Bread.
Leader	In the face of the one who is different, we sometimes fail to recognise you…
All	Lord, open our eyes that we may truly see.
All	Gracious God, expand our hearts beyond their familiar capacity that we may more faithfully serve you and your people. We ask this prayer in the name of Jesus. Amen

Twentieth Sunday in Ordinary Time

Jesus, Our Nourishment

Invitation to Pray

Pause for a few moments of silence and enter more deeply into the presence of God.

> ***Song:*** "O Bread of Heaven," St Alphonsus Liguori,
> tr. Edmund Vaughan

> ***Proclaim the gospel:*** John 6:51-58
> Bread of Life Discourse

Take a few minutes to savour a word, a phrase, a question, or a feeling that rises up in you. Reflect on this quietly or share it aloud. (The other Scripture readings of the day are Proverbs 9:1-6 and Ephesians 5:15-20.)

Invitation to Reflect on the Gospel

The progression through this chapter of John's Gospel is interesting: the multitude is fed, the crowd follows Jesus and the disciples as they go to another location, the crowd questions Jesus about giving them a sign, and Jesus opens up for them that he is the true bread come down from heaven. Though they are scandalised and argumentative, Jesus is very clear and insistent. The ones who were fed by him just the day before, and actually asked to receive this bread (John 6:34), are now scorning Jesus and grumbling about what he is saying.

This could well be a familiar pattern in our own spiritual lives. Things may be in a state of relative calm, or perhaps we're growing in our faith and having new experiences, and a situation develops in which we start to hear things that present a challenge to us. Whether that hearing is through prayer, a friend or family member, a particular preacher, or maybe a current news story, we have an internal sense (a 'gut' feeling) that there is truth in what we hear, but it is not what we *want* to hear, so we resist. Maybe we're being called to a deeper level of faith, trust, giving, or commitment, and we don't feel capable or willing. At times like these our comfort level is being stretched.

The whole of this section of John's Gospel is about the nourishment the Father gives us through Jesus, providing a unique and special way to be connected to him through Jesus' body and blood. This is the mystery that has been central to our Catholic tradition for over two thousand years.

> Whoever eats my flesh and drinks my blood remains in me and I in him. Just as the living Father sent me and I have life because of the Father, so also the one who feeds on me will have life because of me (John 6:56, 57).

This mystery of the Eucharist is the nourishment we need when we are being stretched beyond our "comfort zone." The life of Jesus in the Word and in the consecrated bread and wine will keep us centred during those stretching times of our walk with God.

Invitation to Group Sharing

1. Is the pattern of following Jesus excitedly, asking for something, hearing (or receiving) something else, and then grumbling about it, one that I have seen in my own life? Share with the group.

2. Recall a situation in which you felt challenged to grow in an area in which you didn't really want to grow. How did you respond?

3. What role does the Eucharist play in my life, *especially* when I'm experiencing growth that feels uncomfortable?

4. How are we as a group, an organisation, and/or a parish, being challenged to grow in ways that are unexpected?

Invitation to Act

Determine a specific action (individual or group) that flows from your sharing. This should be your primary consideration. When choosing an individual action, determine what you will do and share it with the group. When choosing a group action, determine who will take responsibility for different aspects of the action. The following are secondary suggestions:

1. Decide to make weekday Mass participation a greater part of your life.

2. Put together a timeline. Remember *specific* instances when you knew, even through hindsight, you were being asked to grow in unexpected ways. As much as possible, write them down chronologically and record what you did to make it through those times. This may be helpful during future challenges.

3. Make spending some quiet time before the Blessed Sacrament one of your prayer practices.

4. Stand in solidarity with a friend or family member who may be experiencing a faith or growth struggle.

5. Contact your Diocesan Pastoral Office to see if there are opportunities for you and/or your parish to contribute time, talent, or treasure in a way that will require a bit of a stretch.

Invitation to Closing Prayer

Give thanks to God (aloud or silently) for insights gained, for desires awakened, for directions clarified, for the gift of one another's openness and sensitivity. Conclude with the following:

Faithful God,

sometimes your way is incomprehensible to us,
so we grumble impatiently;
yet you still feed us,
nurture us,
and call us to yourself.

With humility we offer our gratitude
for the food that is Jesus
who brings us into communion with you.

Through him, may we be more open
to loving you and serving you and those around us. Amen

Twenty-First Sunday in Ordinary Time

Shocking Faith

Invitation to Pray

Pause for a few moments of silence and enter more deeply into the presence of God.

> *Song:* "Come to the Water," John Foley SJ, OCP

> *Proclaim the gospel:* John 6:60-69
> The Words of Eternal Life

Take a few minutes to savour a word, a phrase, a question, or a feeling that rises up in you. Reflect on this quietly or share it aloud. (The other Scripture readings of the day are Joshua 24:1-2a, 15-17, 18b and Ephesians 5:21-32.)

Invitation to Reflect on the Gospel

Today's gospel is the final part of Jesus' instruction about the Living Bread from heaven, and brings to a great crescendo the gospels from the previous four Sundays. Jesus has said some very difficult things that have not been well-received. But today, it is the disciples' murmuring that draws Jesus' attention. They are incredulous, and even sound a bit irritated ("This saying is hard; who can accept it?" [John 6:60]) that Jesus would say what he has about his relationship to the Father, and eating of his flesh and drinking of his blood. Their whole way of thinking, of living, of believing, was being turned upside-down.

Jesus asks two very important questions in his exchange with the disciples; the first is "Does this shock you?" (An earlier translation puts it this way, "Does it shake your faith?")

(John 6:61). We in the 21st century have the grace that two thousand years of faith and tradition bring to us. Accepting Jesus as the bread from heaven may not be as burning an issue for us as it was for those who walked with him. But there *are* issues in the Church, in the world today, and in our lives that may reach into our souls and shake the very foundation of our faith.

The second important question Jesus asks, "Do you also want to leave?" (John 6:67) shows a real vulnerability as Jesus addresses the twelve. He has just poured out who he is, where he comes from, why he has come, how to remain in relationship with him and the Father, and some leave, for it is too hard to bear. Peter meets Jesus' vulnerability with his own. Without fully understanding it, Peter knows there is no place else to turn. God has marked them; to turn away is unthinkable.

We are confronted by these very questions in our daily lives. How we address the issues that shake our faith is greatly influenced by our connection to the Living Bread. The answer to the second question depends upon how we answer the first.

Invitation to Group Sharing

1. What are some Scripture passages, or Church teachings, that are a personal challenge to me? Why do they challenge me?

2. As I recall an experience when I felt my faith was shaken, how did I make it through that difficult time?

3. Have I ever been in a situation when I had to stand up for something that was contrary to what friends or family believed? What did they do? What did I do?

4. Have there been times when I have wanted to leave Jesus; turn my back on my faith? What kept me from leaving? What has Jesus done for me? What can I do for others?

Invitation to Act

Determine a specific action (individual or group) that flows from your sharing. This should be your primary consideration. When choosing an individual action, determine what you will do and share it with the group. When choosing a group action, determine who will take responsibility for different aspects of the action. The following are secondary suggestions:

1. Read the sections of the *Catechism of the Catholic Church* that address the issues in the Church that challenge you. Seek out someone who has been educated in matters of the Church to discuss these issues with.

2. If you know of someone in your family or circle of friends who is facing a particular challenge of faith, make an effort to be supportive. If it is possible, share with him or her a time in your own life when you felt that your faith was being rocked.

3. Develop a parish ministry, such as "Landings," in which alienated Catholics can be nurtured, and through loving effort and concern be brought back into the Church (For more information, contact Pauline Gilbertson on 020 8862 2164 (answerphone), email landingsuk@hotmail.com or see www.landingsuk.org.uk

Invitation to Closing Prayer

Give thanks to God (aloud or silently) for insights gained, for desires awakened, for directions clarified, for the gift of one another's openness and sensitivity. Conclude with the following:

Lord Jesus,

we have come to you
because we have been called
by God our Father.

We are thankful for and humbled by this gift.

To walk with you is very hard at times.
Please help us when we face life's challenges,
for sometimes the temptation to turn away is strong.

Work in our hearts so that we may say as Peter did,
"Master, to whom shall we go?
You have the words of eternal life".
Amen

Twenty-Second Sunday in Ordinary Time

Religious Ritual

Invitation to Pray

Pause for a few moments of silence and enter more deeply into the presence of God.

> *Song:* "The Cry of the Poor," John Foley SJ, OCP

> *Proclaim the gospel:* Mark 7:1-8, 14-15, 21-23
> Tradition of the Elders

Take a few minutes to savour a word, a phrase, a question, or a feeling that rises up in you. Reflect on this quietly or share it aloud. (The other Scripture readings of the day are Deuteronomy 4:1-2, 6-8 and James 1:17-18, 21b-22, 27.)

Invitation to Reflect on the Gospel

This is a challenging gospel on many different levels. For those of us who have not studied ancient Jewish religion, it is hard to understand what is meant by "unclean" and "tradition of the elders." "Unclean" does not mean "soiled." It means that something is ritually defiled. A Jew would be considered ritually unclean if he came into physical contact with a dead body. The "tradition of the elders" refers to a set of practices by which Pharisee teachers meant to help the observant Jew fulfill the law as perfectly as humanly possible. Eventually, for some, these practices took on the same importance as the Law itself, in effect, equating these *human* traditions to the Law that God gave on Mt. Sinai. Jesus' strong rebuke of the religious leaders serves to *return the emphasis to God's Law*, and refocuses the question to inward dispositions and their understanding of external practices. Of course, these were not very popular things to say.

Fast forward to the Church, collectively and individually, more than 2000 years after Jesus spoke these words to certain Pharisees and scribes. This is one of those gospels that can make us squirm in our seats a bit. We are challenged to take a long hard look at how our actions are connected to what we believe. We attend the Sunday Eucharist; we celebrate the Sacrament of Reconciliation regularly; we attend the parish mission, say the rosary, etc. External practices can become routines. Where is our heart while we do these things? What is our attitude? Are we more concerned with being seen at these particular events, than with entering into genuine worship and prayer? How do we treat our family or neighbour after we pass through the church doors and into the outside world? Jesus reminds us that remembering why we do what we do, and doing it with a heart turned toward God, are more important than doing all the correct religious rituals if they are done without conviction and proper intention.

Invitation to Group Sharing

1. In what ways does this gospel challenge me?

2. What specific rites or rituals (religious or personal) are particularly meaningful to me? Why are they meaningful? (An example of a personal ritual may be the way in which your family celebrates Christmas, Easter, birthdays, etc.)

3. Why is it important to have an understanding of the origins of our Catholic rites and rituals? What are the rituals and rites of the Church I do not understand? What will I do to come to a deeper understanding?

Invitation to Act

Determine a specific action (individual or group) that flows from your sharing. This should be your primary consideration. When choosing an individual action, determine what you will do and share it with the group. When choosing a group action, determine who will take responsibility for different aspects of the action. The following are secondary suggestions:

1. Give some thought to and write down a list of personal and religious rituals that are important to you. As much as you are able, write down what you know about their origins.

2. As part of the Dismissal at the end of Mass, the celebrant encourages the congregation to go forward in peace and service of the Lord, to which the assembly responds "Thanks be to God." In the brief moments in which this little ritual occurs, think about how this exchange can be a call or reminder to keep your external practices in line with your inward disposition.

3. Decide how you will live out the words of the Dismissal, for example, teach a child to read, visit the sick, write a letter in support of a justice issue.

4. Ask your priest or parish team member if it would be possible to organise some sort of 'class' for those who wanted to know more about the origins of the rites and rituals that are a part of our Church.

Invitation to Closing Prayer

Give thanks to God (aloud or silently) for insights gained, for desires awakened, for directions clarified, for the gift of one another's openness and sensitivity. Conclude with the following:

Merciful God,

forgive us the times
we enter into worship with ill tempers
and self-righteous attitudes.

When we lose sight of the purpose
for our external practices
challenge us to examine
the disposition of our hearts.

Help us to grow in integrity
that in all our actions
your justice and grace will be known.

With grateful hearts
we offer our prayer through Christ our Lord. Amen

Twenty-Third Sunday in Ordinary Time

The Voice of the Disciple

Invitation to Pray

Pause for a few moments of silence and enter more deeply into the presence of God.

> *Song:* "We Give God Thanks for Those who Knew,"
> Michael Perry, Jubilate Hymns

> *Proclaim the gospel:* Mark 7:31-37
> Healing of a Deaf-Mute

Take a few minutes to savour a word, a phrase, a question, or a feeling that rises up in you. Reflect on this quietly or share it aloud. (The other Scripture readings of the day are Isaiah 35:4-7a and James 2:1-5.)

Invitation to Reflect on the Gospel

Most of us have known what it feels like to have our ears "pop" after descending from a high altitude or recovering from a head cold. What a relief it is, causing us momentarily to marvel at our restored ability to hear. Even the sound of our own voice seems new and wondrous.

Imagine the feelings and sensations experienced by the deaf man in today's gospel. Because of Jesus, he is able to hear for the first time in his life! What a mixture of relief and wonder it must have brought to him. And this is not all that has been healed. The impediment to his speech is instantly taken away as his hearing is given to him. He can now speak in a clear and understandable way.

There is an interesting correlation made in this story between hearing and speech, one that has great significance for those who are to follow Jesus. The invitation to discipleship entails having our own ears "unstopped" so that we can hear the Word of God in our lives. This, in turn, enables us to speak, proclaiming our faith and hope in the One who has healed us. Once able to truly hear, the need and the desire to speak out and testify to our faith is both strong and urgent, a sign that we have indeed answered the call to discipleship.

Jesus was constantly instructing his disciples to listen, to be attentive, to stretch themselves beyond narrow ways of seeing and hearing. This was not easy, especially when they witnessed miracles that brought people their hearing, their sight, their very lives. His admonition to refrain from speaking seems harsh and even unrealistic. Why shouldn't they be allowed to proclaim his wondrous deeds from the rooftops? This gospel may give us a clue. It is essential to listen – to hear *clearly* first – so that one's speech can be understood. Listening can then become a more effective means in preaching the Good News that Jesus has asked us to share with one another.

Invitation to Group Sharing

1. Name a person who seems to have an ability to listen clearly to God's voice. What characterises that ability to hear? How is it connected to his or her ability to speak with truthfulness, faithfulness, and clarity?

2. Share ways in which we can more clearly hear the teachings of the Church.

3. A time in my experience of faith when my own ears were 'unplugged,' when I heard the message of Jesus differently was…. What triggered this?

4. How has being able to hear more clearly given me my voice? How or where do I use it?

Invitation to Act

Determine a specific action (individual or group) that flows from your sharing. This should be your primary consideration. When choosing an individual action, determine what you will do and share it with the group. When choosing a group action, determine who will take responsibility for different aspects of the action. The following are secondary suggestions:

1. Use Psalm 51:17 – *"Lord, open my lips; my mouth will proclaim your praise"* – as a way of continuous. Over the course of the next week, pray it throughout the day as a way to open yourself more fully to the gospel. Next time you gather together as a group, set aside a few minutes to discuss the effect this prayer had in your daily lives.

2. Name someone in your life with whom you have a hard time 'opening your ears.' Think about why it's so difficult to listen to him or her. Decide to be more receptive to what he or she truly has to say about his or her needs, desires, hopes, and fears. Listen for the 'sound of God' through this person.

3. Give voice to your appreciation for the work others do to bring mercy, kindness, justice, and compassion into the world. As a group or as individuals, write a note of affirmation and acknowledgment to them, voicing a particular reason for your admiration of their efforts. This might be addressed to a member of your parish staff. It might be to a school board, city council, charitable board, or other institution created to serve the common good.

Invitation to Closing Prayer

Give thanks to God (aloud or silently) for insights gained, for desires awakened, for directions clarified, for the gift of one another's openness and sensitivity. Conclude with the following:

Jesus,

we put our trust in your healing touch.

Unstop our ears and open our hearts
to your message of justice, love, and compassion,
even when those words challenge us.

Remove the impediments from our speech –
fear, intimidation, apathy, or doubt.

Help us to proclaim our faith loudly
and our love for you with gladness.

We pray all of this in your holy name.

Amen

Twenty-Fourth Sunday in Ordinary Time

"Who Do You Say That I Am?"

Invitation to Pray

Pause for a few moments of silence and enter more deeply into the presence of God.

> *Song:* "Will You Let Me Be Your Servant,"
> Richard Gillard, Scripture in Song

> *Proclaim the gospel:* Mark 8:27-35
> The Messiah's Question

Take a few minutes to savour a word, a phrase, a question, or a feeling that rises up in you. Reflect on this quietly or share it aloud. (The other Scripture readings of the day are Isaiah 50:5-9a and James 2:14-18.)

Invitation to Reflect on the Gospel

"But who do you say that I am?" (Mark 8:29). Peter is quick with an answer to this question. In doing so, he names Jesus as the One, the Messiah, whose coming has been so anticipated. Jesus doesn't commend Peter for his statement of faith. Instead he talks of suffering, which Peter rejects, perhaps in an attempt to make Jesus 'feel better.' Jesus rebukes him quickly and harshly by saying, "Get behind me, Satan" (Mark 8:33). He will not water down or sugarcoat the price of discipleship. It means suffering and there is no other way around it.

This is a puzzling, disturbing passage, especially the rebuke to Peter. Is Peter indeed being a satan (that is, adversary), a tempter, trying to cajole Jesus into seeing things differently? The entire exchange begs another question – "Who do we *want*

Jesus to be?" – A miracle worker? Mr. Fix-It? Santa Claus? Do we want him to be a revolutionary, a prophet, a political leader, a superhero? There are all sorts of ways to make Jesus into the kind of Saviour we want him to be. We can skip over the parts of the gospel that make us uncomfortable. We can put a 'spin' on the Christian message that makes it more suitable for our modern-day lifestyle. We can be tempted to move away from the challenges of discipleship and into a religiosity that is full of 'feel-good' messages of comfort and complacency.

This passage in Mark's Gospel marks an important turning point. Jesus is on the road to Jerusalem, to the cross and suffering. Ultimately it will lead to his Death and his Resurrection. If we are to follow him, are we willing to take on the cross of which he speaks? If so, it will inevitably lead us to consider the question, "Who do you say that I am?" (Mark 8:29). Our answer, as disciples, must come out of faith rather than wishful thinking.

Invitation to Group Sharing

1. Who do people in today's culture seem to want Jesus to be? What indications do I see of this in my home, parish, neighbourhood, school, or workplace?

2. What do I make of Jesus' rebuke to Peter? Does it disturb me? Why?

3. What cross do I bear as I try to follow Jesus? What does it feel like to carry that cross?

4. Read over the last line of the gospel passage one more time. What does it say to me at this point in my life? What questions does it raise for me?

5. Answer Jesus' question, "But who do you say that I am?" (Mark 8:29). How does my response influence my life? How will my response touch others?

Invitation to Act

Determine a specific action (individual or group) that flows from your sharing. This should be your primary consideration. When choosing an individual action, determine what you will do and share it with the group. When choosing a group action, determine who will take responsibility for different aspects of the action. The following are secondary suggestions:

1. Name someone in your life who is bearing a cross that is painful for you to witness. Extend your support and encouragement to this person.

2. Identify one aspect of your life – an attitude, a behaviour, a distraction – that you need to lose in order to be more open to the life God has to share with you. Write it on a card and carry it in your pocket to remind you of your intention to lose it or let it go.

3. Instead of asking God to ease your burdens, pray to him in thanksgiving that he gives you renewed strength to face the challenges that are set in your path.

Invitation to Closing Prayer

Give thanks to God (aloud or silently) for insights gained, for desires awakened, for directions clarified, for the gift of one another's openness and sensitivity. Conclude with the following:

Leader	Lord God, our crosses are heavy, more than we seem able to bear at times. We believe that you have not turned away from us in our struggle to be faithful. Hear us and be our help as we place our needs before you.
Response	"The Lord GOD is my help; who will prove me wrong?"
Leader	It is tempting at times, like Peter, to deny the suffering that is part of our growth in faith. Give us the courage to accept our crosses with hope and grace…R/
Leader	Sometimes it is harder to watch others struggle under the weight of their crosses than to bear our own. Show us how to be supportive, caring and compassionate towards those who are in pain…R/
Leader	The invitation to save our lives through losing them is both mysterious and disturbing. Strengthen us as we let go of aspects of living that ultimately rob us of true life in you…R/
Leader	We ask all of this in the name of Jesus, our Lord and Saviour…R/
All	Amen

Twenty-Fifth Sunday in Ordinary Time

Asking Difficult Questions

Invitation to Pray

Pause for a few moments of silence and enter more deeply into the presence of God.

> ***Song:*** "The Kingdom of God," Bryn Rees

> ***Proclaim the gospel:*** Mark 9:30-37
> Who Is the Greatest?

Take a few minutes to savour a word, a phrase, a question, or a feeling that rises up in you. Reflect on this quietly or share it aloud. (The other Scripture readings of the day are Wisdom 2:12, 17-20 and James 3:16-4:3.)

Invitation to Reflect on the Gospel

"Will this be in the exam?" Such a question grates on the nerves of dedicated teachers who are trying to help students truly learn. It indicates that, rather than grasping the essence of the lesson, the student is focused instead on her or his standing among classmates or on other immediate, self-centred concerns.

In a similar way, Jesus must have felt frustrated after learning of the disciples' discussion over which one will be considered the greatest. Although it might have been tempting to do so, Jesus does not rebuke them. Instead he places in their midst a child – symbol of vulnerability, dependency, and a lack of status or power. In doing so, he invites the disciples to receive those who are humble, unassuming, unexpected, and unlikely to be the ones they'd consider capable of embracing his teachings. It is a touching, warm, and, no doubt, surprising scene, one meant to help the disciples visualise his message more clearly.

The child stands, too, for openness and for an ability to ask difficult questions. After hearing an admittedly difficult teaching from Jesus about his death and Resurrection, the disciples are afraid to ask him anything. While the little child might not have been held back by his or her lack of understanding, the disciples are. Discussing status and prestige is a much safer topic.

To learn from Jesus, the great teacher, we must lay aside our own ambitions, our fears, and sometimes even our own dreams. The Paschal Mystery is central to our Christian belief. Understanding it takes a lifetime and beyond. Opening ourselves to it takes courage and humility. Ultimately, it leads us, not to questions of greatness, but to ones of faith, commitment, and self-effacing love. It is a lesson about dying, one that is hard to hear and understand. For those who are open to receiving it, it is also about life itself, one that will yield the greatest rewards imaginable.

Invitation to Group Sharing

1. Who are the children in our midst today – those who represent vulnerability, dependence, and lack of power or influence? How are they more open than most to the message of Christ?

2. How are we missing the message of Jesus today? What things sideline our understanding of his teachings?

3. What teachings of Jesus frighten me? Why?

4. How can I be more open to the Paschal Mystery on a daily basis?

Invitation to Act

Determine a specific action (individual or group) that flows from your sharing. This should be your primary consideration. When choosing an individual action, determine what you will do and share it with the group. When choosing a group action, determine who will take responsibility for different aspects of the action. The following are secondary suggestions:

1. Name one area in your life in which you would like to be more open to serving others. Take steps to do so.

2. Determine how you can be more attentive to the teachings of Jesus in your daily life. Follow this practice faithfully each day of the coming week.

3. Consider how you can give your time and talent more specifically to helping those who are powerless, vulnerable, or dependent on others for their well-being and safety. This might be through a social justice or outreach project at your parish, through a service provided in your community, or in the way you attend to the children or sick or elderly in your care.

4. Look into the type of services that a local hospice provides to people who are dying and to their carers. Consider how you can volunteer to support their work or how you might promote their services within your parish or community.

Invitation to Closing Prayer

Give thanks to God (aloud or silently) for insights gained, for desires awakened, for directions clarified, for the gift of one another's openness and sensitivity. Conclude with the following:

Jesus,

your words have power
both to challenge and to delight us.
Help us be attentive, to hear
what you are teaching us about death and about life.
Open our eyes to the challenges you put before us.
Show us how to receive the "little ones."
Give us generous spirits and compassionate hearts.
Amen.

Twenty-Sixth Sunday in Ordinary Time

Inclusion and Accountability

Invitation to Pray

Pause for a few moments of silence and enter more deeply into the presence of God.

> *Song:* "Lord, You Give the Great Commission," Jeffrey Rowthorn, Hope Publishing Co
>
> *Proclaim the gospel:* Mark 9:38-43, 45, 47-48
> The Strange Exorcist and
> Temptations to Sin

Take a few minutes to savour a word, a phrase, a question, or a feeling that rises up in you. Reflect on this quietly or share it aloud. (The other Scripture readings of the day are Numbers 11:25-29 and James 5:1-6.)

Invitation to Reflect on the Gospel

The first part of the gospel account contains a classic example of good intentions gone wrong. The disciples have done the hard work of being taught by Jesus on his treks across the countryside. They hear of another person, a stranger, expelling demons in the name of Jesus. Speaking for the group, John tells Jesus of this interloper and, perhaps with a bit of self-inflated pride, also recounts how he and the other disciples tried to stop him.

Imagine his surprise and probable indignation when Jesus stands in support of this strange exorcist. If the work is being done in his name, he states, then this stranger is unlikely to be against them. Rather than cast this person aside, Jesus embraces him and affirms the work he is doing. It's a strong statement of inclusion, of paying attention to the intent behind the work of the stranger. John and the other disciples have learned yet another lesson about the reign of God.

The passage continues in another, seemingly contradictory direction. Jesus talks, rather brutally, of dealing harshly with the parts of ourselves – hands, feet, eyes – that cause us to 'stumble.' It is a disturbing, gruesome passage that stands in sharp contrast to the understanding way Jesus deals with the strange exorcist.

Can this really be what he means? Are we to mutilate ourselves in an effort to keep from sinning? Not quite.

Scriptural references to parts of the human body are often made in reference to the community, not to the individual. In other words, Jesus may be talking about cutting off parts of the community who are against him and who mislead others, those who are unlikely to know any better, astray in their faith. The cost of discipleship is extreme. It requires total commitment and a single-heartedness as extolled in the Beatitudes. Anything less is not worth holding on to.

In today's terms, we might call this *accountability*. On the one hand, it means including those who, although not officially sanctioned through education, credentials, or parish membership, are doing the work of Christ. Even well-intentioned efforts to safeguard the integrity of the community may not always be what God would have us do.

On the other hand, it means holding one another accountable for the ways we may lead others astray. This might be done more through neglect than active intent. It might be through becoming complacent, lazy, cynical, suspicious, jealous, or petty.

Whatever the reason, we cannot lose sight of our mission as Christians, one that should unite us in a common purpose. Jesus' message is one of life and death. As such, it is to be taken to heart. Nothing else will do.

Invitation to Group Sharing

1. Who are the 'little ones' Jesus is referring to in the gospel? Who would this refer to in modern society?

2. What do I make of Jesus saying, "Whoever is not against us is for us" (Mark 9:40)? Who constitutes this group today?

3. How have I demonstrated recently that I am 'for' Jesus? Name one or two specific signs of this.

4. Name some of the different ways we, as individuals and as a faith community, can be held accountable for our beliefs, our actions, and our commitment to discipleship.

Invitation to Act

Determine a specific action (individual or group) that flows from your sharing. This should be your primary consideration. When choosing an individual action, determine what you will do and share it with the group. When choosing a group action, determine who will take responsibility for different aspects of the action. The following are secondary suggestions:

1. Examine the things within your own life that need to be cut off or plucked out in order to make you a more faithful disciple. Determine what it will take to do this and do something about it.

2. Name one way you can deepen your commitment to your faith in Jesus in the next week, month, or year. Resolve to follow through on your idea.

3. Pray for those who are struggling to carry out the work of Christ in the midst of opposition or resistance from fellow Christians. Use the Beatitudes (Matthew 5:1-11) to help deepen your reflection.

Invitation to Closing Prayer

Give thanks to God (aloud or silently) for insights gained, for desires awakened, for directions clarified, for the gift of one another's openness and sensitivity. Conclude with the following:

Leader   Let us take time to pray together reflecting on
         the spirit of the Beatitudes (Matthew 5:6-8).
         May it be a time to reflect upon ways
         to hold ourselves and others to the faith
         we profess in Jesus Christ.

Reader 1   Blessed are those who hunger and thirst
           for righteousness...

Reader 2   ...for they will be satisfied.

[Pause]

All   Generous God, bless those who are zealous
           in their quest for justice and keep them
           on a path that is always directed toward you.
           Fill them and us with a desire to
           see your 'little ones' cared for
           and treated with dignity and respect.

Reader 1   Blessed are the merciful...

Reader 2   ....for they will be shown mercy.

[Pause]

All   Merciful God, bless those who recognise your
           steadfast love in all aspects of their lives and who
           extend themselves to others in gentle acts
           of mercy and compassion.
           Bring them and us comfort
           when we feel most desperate and alone.

Reader 1   Blessed are the pure in heart...

Reader 2   ....for they will see God.

[Pause]

All   All-powerful God, bless those
           who are fervent in their faith.
           Reveal yourself to them and to us
           through every aspect of our lives.

Leader   We offer these prayers with confidence
           through the Holy Spirit and
           in the name of Jesus, the Lord.

All   Amen

Twenty-Seventh Sunday in Ordinary Time

Marriage, Divorce, and Commitment

Invitation to Pray

Pause for a few moments of silence and enter more deeply into the presence of God.

> *Song:* "Blest Are They," David Haas, GIA

> *Proclaim the gospel:* Mark 10:2-16
> Teaching About Divorce; Blessing the Little Children

Take a few minutes to savour a word, a phrase, a question, or a feeling that rises up in you. Reflect on this quietly or share it aloud. (The other Scripture readings of the day are Genesis 2:18-24 and Hebrews 2:9-11.)

Invitation to Reflect on the Gospel

The first reading for this Sunday is the account of the creation of Adam and Eve. It is a story of Eve's equality with Adam. She is not created from the earth as the animals are, but from the side of Adam. She is, he proclaims, "bone of my bones/ and flesh of my flesh" (Genesis 2:23).

The first part of the gospel reading is one that might make some people uncomfortable. Proclaimed at Mass, one might wonder how it affects those who have been touched by the pain of divorce. Does it strike them and others as unduly harsh, condemning, or unyielding?

Jesus departs from the Law in a radical way when he says that the consequences of divorce are the same for both the man and the woman. He 'levels the playing field' and holds the man to be as accountable for a break in relationship as the woman. Divorce is equally injurious to both women and men and it runs counter to God's intent of unity and equality in marriage.

The marriage vow itself makes clear that the husband and wife may expect a good measure of difficulty and distress in their years together. It will not be easy to love each other "as Christ loved the church" (Ephesians 5:25). But the vowed partners know that the image of marital love is an earthly expression of God's love for us. The unity of marriage is meant to be unbreakable as God's love for us is unconditional. Husband and wife are to be examples to all of God's faithfulness and mercy, patience and generosity. This great responsibility should never be taken lightly. The love of husband and wife is the earthly image of Christ's love for his people.

What does this say to us today? Certainly our understanding of marriage as an equal partnership has deepened over the centuries, even if it has not been totally realised in certain cultures or individual households. We may have also come to a deeper understanding that not all marriages are *able* to stay intact. People change or they sometimes marry for the wrong reasons. Life's burdens and tragedies may put more pressure on a relationship than it can handle and it cracks apart under that weight.

No one knows as intimately as the person who has experienced divorce how painful it is. Despite contemporary attempts to make light of it – even to make a joke out of it – divorce signifies a separation between two people who have vowed to stay together. While the vocation to Christian marriage calls one to a faithful and permanent commitment, there are marriages that do end painfully and without the hope of new life. A ministry to the separated and divorced remains an important expression of the compassion and care of Jesus Christ. We are always called to treat each other with respect and loving concern.

What matters is that we take our commitments seriously and hold on to ideals as the good that God intends for us. We recognise God as the one who, as Creator of us all, sees most fully into the human heart.

The gospel concludes with the endearing account of Jesus and the children whom he reaches out to embrace despite the objections of his disciples. Perhaps the line in the entire passage that merits deepest attention is this: "Amen, I say to you, whoever does not accept the kingdom of God like a child will not enter it" (Mark 10:15).

The child is the one without guile, the one who is not weighed down by guilt, blame, shame, or feelings of inadequacy. The child is the one who, after falling down, gets up and tries again. The child stands as a model of trust and openness for all.

Our commitments to one another will have to endure similar ups and downs. Even though few of us will fully reach the ideal – the bar held high – we can always hope, like the child, that God's love will hold us together in dignity and mutual respect. We can trust that, even when we fail, God's forgiveness and compassion will be extended in full to us.

Invitation to Group Sharing

1. How can people who have gone through a separation or divorce find hope in this gospel?

2. Is there a relationship in my life that needs attention? How equal or unequal do I feel in it? What are some ways I can bolster the relationship? What part does faith play in my relationship?

3. How can I be more open to receiving the kingdom of God like a child?

4. How can I effectively reach out to those who have been touched by an abortion, a violent crime?

Invitation to Act

Determine a specific action (individual or group) that flows from your sharing. This should be your primary consideration. When choosing an individual action, determine what you will do and share it with the group. When choosing a group action, determine who will take responsibility for different aspects of the action. The following are secondary suggestions:

1. Pray for those who are having trouble with their relationships – for married couples, for those who are in the process of separation or divorce. Reflect upon the pain in their lives and ask for God's healing and comforting love to be made present to them.

2. Pay attention to children's attitudes toward life, toward God. Learn from them what it means to accept the Kingdom of God.

3. Reach out to someone who is in a painful relationship or who has recently separated or divorced.

4. Consult your Diocesan Pastoral Affairs office about how you could be involved in marriage preparation programmes.

5. Become involved in the pro-life movement in your parish or diocese.

6. Pray for those who are unborn and those struggling with the pain of abortion.

Invitation to Closing Prayer

Give thanks to God (aloud or silently) for insights gained, for desires awakened, for directions clarified, for the gift of one another's openness and sensitivity. Conclude with the following:

God of love and compassion,

it is not always easy to hear what you expect of us.
It is difficult to live out our commitments
and sometimes we fail.

Help us to trust in your forgiveness and understanding,
especially when we fail to live up to the ideals
you place before us.

We believe in your goodness and mercy.
We place ourselves and all those who struggle to remain
faithful in their relationships into your compassionate care.
Give us the heart, the mind, and the spirit of the little child
who looks to you clear-eyed and hopeful.

We pray all of this in the name of our Lord,
Jesus Christ.

Amen

Twenty-Eighth Sunday in Ordinary Time

The Cost of Discipleship

Invitation to Pray

Pause for a few moments of silence and enter more deeply into the presence of God.

> *Song:* "My God, Accept My Heart this Day,"
> Matthew Bridges

> *Proclaim the gospel:* Mark 10:17-30
> The Rich Young Man

Take a few minutes to savour a word, a phrase, a question, or a feeling that rises up in you. Reflect on this quietly or share it aloud. (The other Scripture readings of the day are Wisdom 7:7-11 and Hebrews 4:12-13.)

Invitation to Reflect on the Gospel

This gospel follows the theme of the extraordinary cost of discipleship that has been developed over the past few weeks. This familiar passage in which a young man earnestly seeks to follow Jesus is one that is both challenging and intriguing. The would-be disciple's question: "What must I do to inherit eternal life?" (Mark 10:17), reiterates the necessity of keeping the commandments. This is just the starting point for those who would make a commitment to discipleship, however. Jesus' demand that the young man sell what he has and give it to the poor is beyond what he feels he can do. He goes away grieving and we are left to wonder if he ever did make the commitment he so eagerly sought.

The whole episode raises many questions. Does it mean we must live in poverty to follow Jesus? Does it mean we are to have no lasting human relationships or that we are to flee from those relationships in order to take on the role of the disciple? Peter once again takes on the role of questioner for the rest of the disciples. "We have given up everything and followed you" (Mark 10:28). "What more do you expect of us?" he seems to be asking.

Following this selection is the third teaching in Mark about Jesus' passion and death. Those who are willing to follow in his path are opening themselves up to persecution. The way of the cross is one that entails suffering. There is no other way around it.

This is a gospel that holds great potential for abuse through misinterpretation. It can lead to a misguided notion that abandoning one's commitments is the path to true enlightenment. Rather than providing us with an excuse to be irresponsible, its deeper point might be one of *attachment*. Growing in faith is a constant process of leaving our comfort zones. Possessions can weigh us down when we spend more time protecting them than using them for the good of all. Our relationships with family and friends can stifle our ability to grow if they are not freeing us to become more compassionate and open to life.

Our Christian story is filled with examples of saints who learned how to move forward, who detached themselves from people and things that hampered their commitment to Christ. These role models used their possessions or power to help those in need. They did not let their relationships with family, friends, or colleagues pull them back into ruts and routines. Their zeal and passion for Christ impelled them to keep moving. Such commitment not only seems heroic, it seems miraculous – much like a camel squeezing itself through the eye of a needle (Mark 10:25). God alone can make it happen.

Invitation to Group Sharing

1. When the young man asks how he can inherit eternal life, Jesus regards him with tenderness. How can I act like Jesus?

2. How might the words in this gospel challenge me to rethink or deepen my stance on the Church's teachings on life issues such as euthanasia or abortion?

3. How do my possessions and/or relationships hold me back from making a wholehearted commitment to Christ?

4. The second reading of the day is from the Letter to the Hebrews: "...the word of God is living and effective, sharper than any two-edged sword..." (Hebrews 4:12). How is today's gospel like that two-edged sword?

5. What 'things' do I own? What do I need to 'sell' – literally or figuratively – in order to follow Jesus? How will I do this?

Invitation to Act

Determine a specific action (individual or group) that flows from your sharing. This should be your primary consideration. When choosing an individual action, determine what you will do and share it with the group. When choosing a group action, determine who will take responsibility for different aspects of the action. The following are secondary suggestions:

1. Name one area of your life that has become a comfort zone, something that is holding you back from full discipleship. How can you let it go?

2. Commit yourself to praying for and helping those who struggle with sincerity to follow Jesus but who, like the young man, find it difficult to let go of their perceived security in order to do so.

3. Do some housekeeping. Go through a wardrobe or dresser drawer this week and sort out the things that are taking up space. Donate the items to a charitable organisation or a person in need, and savour the feeling of relief that comes from a bit of 'downsizing.'

4. Contact Life or SPUC and inform yourself and your small group about ways you can help foster pro-life activities. As a group commit to one activity that fosters life.

Invitation to Closing Prayer

Give thanks to God (aloud or silently) for insights gained, for desires awakened, for directions clarified, for the gift of one another's openness and sensitivity. Conclude with the following:

Response   I prayed, and prudence was given me;
I pleaded, and the spirit of Wisdom came to me.

Leader   Father, Creator and giver of life,
help us to embrace the gifts you have
given to us and show us how to use them
generously in service to your people…R/

Leader   Jesus, Saviour and Redeemer,
show us how to let go of those aspects
of our lives that inhibit our growth,
make us timid and fearful,
and keep us from seeing
the larger possibilities that lie before us…R/

242

Leader	Spirit of wisdom and love,
	fill our hearts with passion for your word
	and a zeal for your work…R/

Leader	May all good things come to us
	as a result of Wisdom's company and true
	riches be ours through God's abundant grace.

All	Glory to the Father,
	and to the Son,
	and to the Holy Spirit,
	as it was in the beginning, is now,
	and will be forever. Amen

Twenty-Ninth Sunday in Ordinary Time

Servant Leadership

Invitation to Pray

Pause for a few moments of silence and enter more deeply into the presence of God.

> *Song:* "The Servant King," Graham Kendrick,
> Kingsway's Thankyou Music

> *Proclaim the gospel:* Mark 10:35-45
> The Request of James and John

Take a few minutes to savour a word, a phrase, a question, or a feeling that rises up in you. Reflect on this quietly or share it aloud. (The other Scripture readings of the day are Isaiah 53:10-11 and Hebrews 4:14-16.)

Invitation to Reflect on the Gospel

James and John are portrayed here in a rather unflattering way. Their request to sit in positions of glory – "one at your right [hand] and the other at your left" (Mark 10:37) – seems pompous, self-serving, and even childish. Jesus is patient with them as he challenges their lack of comprehension about the ramifications of such a request. The whole scene provides an opportunity for him to teach all twelve about servant leadership.

This passage forms one of the most well-known and paradoxical parts of Jesus' message. Those who would place themselves first, who seek to become powerful and to use that power over others, will be made last in the reign of God. Those who serve others in humility and kindness will be made first. The cost of such service is high, requiring one to give his or her life for others.

Is there anything more difficult to witness than the suffering of an innocent person?

- The image of a father trying vainly to protect his young son from gunfire on a war-torn street
- The young mother whose life is cruelly shortened by the onset of cancer
- The commuters caught in the terrorist attacks in London, July 2005.

These images assault our sensibilities, dredging up an anguished cry of "why?" from deep within. Such suffering appears senseless, cruel, out-of-sync with the way God's justice and mercy *should* be working. As if it is not hard enough to hear of such suffering in the world, Jesus seems to be saying we have to be open to it as well.

Most of us, in our attempts to live our faith, will not meet an end like many of the early disciples. We won't be crucified, tortured, or beheaded as we stand up for our beliefs. What we are asked to do, however, will still take its toll on our hearts and spirits. Living out the gospel could require us to care for a loved one with a long-term illness, to enter into a lengthy process of forgiving someone who has betrayed us, to stretch ourselves to a point of exhaustion in order to reach out to those in need. Surrounded as we are by a culture that champions our 'rights' – to sue, to place blame, and to make ourselves victims – servant leadership can be an enormous challenge.

Jesus himself leads the way. For those who try to follow him, however imperfectly, the image of his Passion and Death is a continual reminder of the faithfulness and love that is a requisite part of discipleship. The examples of the Twelve also inspire above. Despite their lack of understanding and their childish requests, they went on to do great things in humble ways. Their reward, in the end, may have been much more than they ever dreamed possible. Such is the hope of the believer.

Invitation to Group Sharing

1. How can I respond like Jesus when others make self-serving requests?

2. Recall a time when you had to serve another. What did it cost? What rewards, if any, were there?

3. What can I learn from pain and suffering? How can I respond as Jesus did?

4. Individually or as a group, how can I or we reach out to someone who is 'suffering wrongly'?

Invitation to Act

Determine a specific action (individual or group) that flows from your sharing. This should be your primary consideration. When choosing an individual action, determine what you will do and share it with the group. When choosing a group action, determine who will take responsibility for different aspects of the action. The following are secondary suggestions:

1. Reach out to someone who is suffering, a prisoner unjustly sentenced to death or incarceration, a cancer patient, or a person living in poverty. Brainstorm ways in which you can help through direct or indirect action.

2. Become involved in the pro-life activities of your parish or diocese. Make plans to join any large-scale organised events that support the pro-life cause.

3. Commit yourself to praying daily for someone you know or know about who is suffering or struggling to live out his or her faith in service to others. Commit to praying for someone who is tempted with abortion as a solution.

4. Find out more about 'Basic Caring Communities' - providing community support for past prisoners. For more details contact Fr. Malachy Keegan (Principal Roman Catholic Chaplain to Prisons) at malachy.keegan@hmps.gsi.gov.uk

Invitation to Closing Prayer

Give thanks to God (aloud or silently) for insights gained, for desires awakened, for directions clarified, for the gift of one another's openness and sensitivity. Conclude with the following:

Leader Let us lift up our prayers to God
     in a spirit of faith and trust.
     For those who suffer under the weight
     of physical pain or emotional hurt,
     that they will experience comfort and healing,
     we pray to the Lord.

Response Lord, hear our prayer.

Leader For those who serve others humbly, in homes,
     hospitals, prisons, schools, and places of worship,
     that they will be strengthened in their work,
     we pray to the Lord...R/

Leader	For those who exercise power over others through business, military service, and public office, that they will be given the gift of servant leadership, we pray to the Lord…R/
Leader	*[Invite the group to offer prayers for specific intentions.]* We pray to the Lord…R/
Leader	We lift up these prayers to you, God of mercy and justice. Give us the strength and the courage to seek true greatness through our willingness to serve others. Help us with our own struggles and ease the pain in our lives. We ask this in the name of Jesus, the Suffering Servant whom we seek to follow.
All	Amen

Thirtieth Sunday in Ordinary Time

"What Do You Want Me to Do for You?"

Invitation to Pray

Pause for a few moments of silence and enter more deeply into the presence of God.

> *Song:* "Take My Life and Let It Be,"
> Frances R. Havergal

> *Proclaim the gospel:* Mark 10:46-52
> The Healing of Blind Bartimaeus

Take a few minutes to savour a word, a phrase, a question, or a feeling that rises up in you. Reflect on this quietly or share it aloud. (The other Scripture readings of the day are Jeremiah 31:7-9 and Hebrews 5:1-6.)

Invitation to Reflect on the Gospel

Mark's account of the healing of Bartimaeus is one filled with poignant meaning and challenge. It opens with a picture of Bartimaeus, a blind beggar, sitting by the side of the road. A crowd of people surrounds him, all straining to see Jesus as he passes by. Bartimaeus calls out from his lowly place and the crowd attempts to shout him down in order to keep him quiet. He's just a beggar. What right does he have to cry for help? Unfazed, he calls again, pleading for mercy. Jesus hears him above the din of the crowd and now the people around Bartimaeus change their tune. Be brave, they tell him, as if he hasn't already shown his courage and determination.

Jesus, upon meeting him, asks very simply, "What do you

want me to do for you?" (Mark 10:51). It is the question of a servant leader, something he has been trying to teach his disciples for quite some time. "Master, I want to see," Bartimaeus answers (Mark 10:51). It is a simple response, one coming directly from the heart.

If Jesus were asking that same question of us, how would we respond? Most of us could come up with a dozen replies right off the top of our heads. After all, there are all sorts of voices in our lives that tell us what we need. Having a new car, a different hair colour, a better brand of toothpaste, a certain beer – these will bring status, beauty, confidence, and fun. Voices of peers, family members, colleagues, and self-help experts tell us other things. We should want to be popular, responsible, successful, or "whole."

Internal voices can be even more confusing. Sometimes these attempt to stifle the desires of our hearts. We tell ourselves we're not good enough, smart enough, or attractive enough to ask for anything. Doubt, fear, anger, apathy, or just plain weariness can muddy our internal vision, keeping us blinded to what it is we most want Jesus to do for us.

How then do we get to the heart of the matter? How do we respond to Jesus' question?

Once summoned by Jesus, Bartimaeus casts off his cloak and hurries forward to meet him. The cloak of a poor beggar had to have been a prized possession, one of the only things he owned. Yet he casts it off and moves forward unencumbered by it or anything else.

So it is with us. In order to truly understand what we most want, we have to cast aside the distractions that clutter our lives. This often happens *for* us, usually against our own will. Grief and loss, disease and disability strip away the superficial concerns of our lives and lay bare our hearts. It is then we are most able – and most free – to name the sort of healing we ache for Jesus to do for us.

At the end of the story, Bartimaeus is told it is his strong and unwavering faith that has saved him. Deferring credit for a miracle, Jesus sees way beyond the physical restoration of sight given to this poor man. Bartimaeus has received much more than he could have ever hoped for, and his joyful exuberance in following Jesus afterwards bears witness to this.

Perhaps our own blindness, our sinfulness, can best be faced through the sacrament of penance and reconciliation. The sacrament enables us to face our need for change through the desire to make amends.

It takes faith to cry out, to express our deepest desires, and to cast aside our own cloaks of comfort and security. It takes faith to believe God already knows what lies deep within our hearts. It takes faith to trust that the answer we so long for is already being formed in ways we may not anticipate. It takes faith – and a bit of vision.

Invitation to Group Sharing

1. What external forces work to keep us from knowing what we truly want from Jesus?

2. What internal voices do the same? How are we to contend with these forces?

3. What do I want Jesus to do for me?

4. What sort of "cloaks" can we cast aside in order to understand what lies deep within our hearts? How can the sacrament of penance and reconciliation free me to cast aside my cloaks?

Invitation to Act

Determine a specific action (individual or group) that flows from your sharing. This should be your primary consideration. When choosing an individual action, determine what you will do and share it with the group. When choosing a group action, determine who will take responsibility for different aspects of the action. The following are secondary suggestions:

1.   Name the "crowds" you belong to – committees, workplaces, clubs, institutions – that sometimes suppress the expression of the needs of individuals. Become a voice of encouragement and support within each of them.

2.   Recall someone you know who is struggling to express his or her own heartfelt desires for healing or restoration in his or her life. Reach out to this person. Help him or her open up to the saving, loving touch of Jesus.

3.   Take a look at the way in which the social systems in your area listen to the felt needs of the poor and disabled and unborn. Be a voice for those in need through the way you vote, volunteer, or otherwise participate in the life of your community.

Invitation to Closing Prayer

Give thanks to God (aloud or silently) for insights gained, for desires awakened, for directions clarified, for the gift of one another's openness and sensitivity. Conclude with the following:

> Loving and generous Father,
> You alone know the workings of the human heart.
> Show us how to listen to the yearnings
> we have deep within ourselves.
> Remove from our midst any impediments or distractions
> that block us from turning to you in our need.
> Open us up to your healing touch
> and your bounteous goodness.
> Then we shall be free to rejoice,
> along with those faithful ones of ages past,
> in your generosity and in your power to heal and console.
>
> We offer this prayer and all of our deepest needs
> in the name of your Son, our Lord Jesus Christ.
> Amen

Thirty-First Sunday in Ordinary Time

The Greatest Commandments

Invitation to Pray

Pause for a few moments of silence and enter more deeply into the presence of God.

> *Song:* "Blest Are They," David Haas, GIA

> *Proclaim the gospel:* Mark 12:28b-34
> The First Commandment

Take a few minutes to savour a word, a phrase, a question, or a feeling that rises up in you. Reflect on this quietly or share it aloud. (The other Scripture readings of the day are Deuteronomy 6:2-6 and Hebrews 7:23-28.)

Invitation to Reflect on the Gospel

It's hard to imagine how many love songs have been composed over the centuries. Most have to do with romantic love and the exquisite longing and preoccupation one has for his or her beloved. The locus of the song is usually the heart, which aches and breaks, pines and whines, soars and roars with love for the other.

This gospel contains a message that itself is at the heart of Jewish and Christian belief and practice. It is one of the earliest lessons we learn in religious education: love God and love your neighbour as yourself. It seems so simple and straightforward; yet it may be the most challenging part of living our faith.

As we look at the state of our world and at human history, it is evident that loving our neighbour as we love ourselves is still far from being realised in its fullest sense. Whether we're shooting at one another on a battlefield or assaulting one another with abusive language in our homes, it says as much about the way we regard ourselves as it does the other person. Love is easier to sing about than live.

Around this time of year we celebrate the great feast of All Saints. It is a day to honour all those holy men and women of God who lived their lives trying to remain faithful to these two great commandments. The reason they achieved sainthood is because they focused on the first – and greatest – of the commandments. Their very lives were a love song devoted to God whom they sought to know and embrace. Animated by such love for the Creator, one must extend that love outward to others, especially those who seem most unlovable.

The example of these holy people can serve as both an inspiration and a challenge to us. Their lives were not lived out evenly or easily and their quest for God often led them down difficult paths. Loving God brought many of them to a point of conversion, of turning their lives around. While some had visions and experienced extraordinary phenomena such as ecstasies, such expressions of Christian life have been neither central nor common. Love of God and neighbour in humble service remains forever the pulse beat of the Christian vocation.

To love God is to give rise to the song in our hearts, one that calls us into deeper relationship with the One who has first loved us. It is a love that, by its very nature, affects the way we stand in relationship with others. Such love exposes us at times to the very raw edges of life. It opens us up to pain as well as to joy. It makes us vulnerable and ready to give. It deepens and stretches our capacity to care, to reach out, to see ourselves and others as lovable in the eyes of God. It is a love truly worth singing about.

Invitation to Group Sharing

1. What does it mean to love God
    with my whole heart?
    with all my soul?
    with all my mind?
    with all my strength?

2. Think of someone whom you are having a difficult time loving. How can my love for God help me in this relationship?

3. What song do I hold in my heart? How is it calling me into deeper relationship with God?

4. Loving oneself is sometimes a bigger challenge than loving others. In what ways have I neglected my own needs? How will I tend to them more lovingly within the coming week?

Invitation to Act

Determine a specific action (individual or group) that flows from your sharing. This should be your primary consideration. When choosing an individual action, determine what you will do and share it with the group. When choosing a group action, determine who will take responsibility for different aspects of the action. The following are secondary suggestions:

1. Take time over the next several days to ask God for help in being more loving toward a person you find difficult to love.

2. Examine the ways in which your participation in the Eucharist is enhancing the love you have for God. Consider new forms of participation by becoming a reader, extraordinary minister of communion, greeter, or catechist.

3. Put your love for your neighbour into practice. Take time this week to write to or spend time with someone who is homeless, or someone who has lost a loved one or is suffering in any way.

4. Be aware of the Church's stance on euthanasia and be ready to speak about it, if called upon.

Invitation to Closing Prayer

Give thanks to God (aloud or silently) for insights gained, for desires awakened, for directions clarified, for the gift of one another's openness and sensitivity. Conclude with the following:

Pray St. Paul's reflection on love in a contemplative way. Give one line to each person and then thoughtfully read, ending with everyone joining for the last verse.

1. "If I speak in human and angelic tongues,
   but do not have love,
   I am a resounding gong or a clashing cymbal.

2. And if I have the gift of prophecy,
   and comprehend all mysteries and all knowledge;
   if I have all faith so as to move mountains,
   but do not have love, I am nothing.

3. If I give away everything I own,
    and if I hand my body over so that I may boast,
    but do not have love, I gain nothing.

4. Love is patient; love is kind.
    It is not jealous, [love] is not pompous,
    it is not inflated, it is not rude,

5. it does not seek its own interests, it is not quick-tem-
    pered,
    it does not brood over injury,
    it does not rejoice over wrongdoing
    but rejoices with the truth.

6. It bears all things, believes all things,
    hopes all things, endures all things.

7. Love never fails.…

All …So faith, hope, love remain, these three;
    but the greatest of these is love."
    (1 Corinthians 13:1-8a, 13)

Thirty-Second Sunday in Ordinary Time

A Widow's Gift

Invitation to Pray

Pause for a few moments of silence and enter more deeply into the presence of God.

> *Song:* "The Cry of the Poor," John Foley, SJ, OCP

> *Proclaim the gospel:* Mark 12:38-44
> Scribes and a Widow

Take a few minutes to savour a word, a phrase, a question, or a feeling that rises up in you. Reflect on this quietly or share it aloud. (The other Scripture readings of the day are 1 Kings 17:10-16 and Hebrews 9:24-28.)

Invitation to Reflect on the Gospel

This passage from Mark offers stark contrasts between the way people give. Jesus points out to his disciples the strutting, pompous behaviour of some of the scribes. Entrusted with the important task of interpreting Jewish law, these men held a great deal of power. Jesus notes the ways in which they abuse it and the resultant consequences. "They devour the houses of widows and, as a pretext, recite lengthy prayers. They will receive a very severe condemnation" (Mark 12:40).

The second account concerns a poor widow who puts two small copper coins – the smallest form of currency in circulation at that time – into the temple treasury. Her gift, Jesus notes, is great indeed, because it represents everything she has. It is a gift given not out of her surplus, but out of her need.

Calling his disciples around him, Jesus uses the widow as an example of humility and generosity. It is clearly what he expects of those who would follow him.

The widow serves as a symbol of one who is without resources or a safety net to support her. Being so destitute, her tiny offering is one that puts her whole life in jeopardy. As a widow she is dependent upon public charity for her most basic needs. She has no one to call on to pay her bills, no job to bring in a steady flow of income. Giving away just two coins is an enormous act of generosity and trust.

What induces a person to take such a risk, to give so much? Following, as this does, the gospel account about the two great Commandments, the answer could only be love. The group of scribes whom Jesus is observing knows the Mosaic Law in great depth. What they have not grasped, however, is its spirit, and this shows itself in their actions and attitudes. This results in very real and devastating consequences in the lives of others.

A poor woman, without status and without power, comes forward to give away most of what she has. She does not stop to question whether the temple officials are spending the money wisely nor does she attach any strings to her donation. She gives because it is right to do so. That it will cost her greatly does not deter her.

Acts of simple generosity still have the power to touch us profoundly. It is not just the gift – the handful of pennies – that moves us. It is the attitude of those who, like the poor widow, give because she or he could do no less. It simply isn't in their hearts to do so.

Invitation to Group Sharing

1. How does this gospel passage impact my faith?

2. When have I experienced a time when I gave out of my need as opposed to my surplus? What motivated me to do this? What did it cost me?

3. The Gospel of Mark speaks to us about giving monetarily. In what other ways can we use our resources to alleviate the pain of others?

Invitation to Act

Determine a specific action (individual or group) that flows from your sharing. This should be your primary consideration. When choosing an individual action, determine what you will do and share it with the group. When choosing a group action, determine who will take responsibility for different aspects of the action. The following are secondary suggestions:

1. This Sunday's readings start with the account of another poor widow. Take some time to read and reflect upon 1 Kings 17:10-16. In order to be open to God's ability to provide for your greatest needs, use this passage to help you through any area of uncertainty you are experiencing now.

2. Take time to examine your charitable contributions and where and how you give of your time, talent, and treasure. Give consideration to the possibility of being more generous, especially to those in need.

3. Volunteer to provide rides for the elderly to Mass on weekends or to parish activities. In doing so, you provide an opportunity for them to stay connected with their parish family.

Invitation to Closing Prayer

Give thanks to God (aloud or silently) for insights gained, for desires awakened, for directions clarified, for the gift of one another's openness and sensitivity. Conclude with the following:

> Gracious God,
> everything we have is a gift from you.
>
> Open our hearts so that we, like the poor widow,
> may give to others with a spirit of generosity and humility.
> Give us a thirst for justice and help us to recognize
> our own capacity for compassion and caring.
>
> We ask this through Jesus Christ,
> who gave his own life out of love for us. Amen

Thirty-Third Sunday in Ordinary Time

Attentive Hope

Invitation to Pray

Pause for a few moments of silence and enter more deeply into the presence of God.

> *Song:* "Canticle of the Sun," Marty Haugen, GIA

> *Proclaim the gospel:* Mark 13:24-32
> The Coming of the Son of Man

Take a few minutes to savour a word, a phrase, a question, or a feeling that rises up in you. Reflect on this quietly or share it aloud. (The other Scripture readings of the day are Daniel 12:1-3 and Hebrews 10:11-14, 18.)

Invitation to Reflect on the Gospel

"The heavens are telling the glory of God, and all creation is shouting for joy."

The opening lines of this session's suggested song speak of the joyful and exuberant signs of God's glory shown through nature. It provides a marked contrast to the opening lines in the gospel passage. Sometimes referred to as the "Little Apocalypse," the words of Jesus paint an entirely different picture of the days to come. These include frightful and mysterious images of stars falling out of the sky, and the sun and moon no longer giving the earth light and warmth.

Apocalyptic literature is fraught with such imagery. Usually written for a people who have been or are going through times of persecution, the message is intended to give hope by encouraging believers to trust in the power and might of God. So it is in Mark's Gospel. The writer is attempting to cool the fears of the followers of Jesus who are experiencing persecution for their beliefs and practice.

To contemporary readers, these words may seem far from comforting. In a day of instant access to global events, such images may also seem a bit mundane. After all, we can usually take our pick on the evening news of stories that routinely feature terrifying footage of war, earthquakes, car accidents, and fires. Television 'calamity' programmes use natural disasters and street crimes to entertain us. We live in an age when we are not only likely to misinterpret signs of the Second Coming, we're liable to be dulled to the magnitude of them while we sit gazing blankly at a television screen.

Tucked in the middle of Mark's Gospel is a gentle, homely reference to a fig tree going through its yearly cycle of growth. Attentiveness to the signs around us that are most immediate and ordinary may yield the greatest insights into what lies ahead. The voice of the prophet constantly warns us to see beyond what is placed squarely in front of us. In our media-saturated age, it may be a greater challenge than ever to spot the signs that Christ is coming again and anew, to bring peace, to shake up heaven and earth. As Christians our lives are rooted in the hope of better days to come. Attentiveness is mixed with anticipation of the day, unknown by all except the Father, when the reign of God is fully realised in our midst. We cannot even begin to grasp what that will look like. We can, however, try to stay alert and aware, grounded in the faith that whatever tribulations may come our way, there are greater days ahead. Then we will join with all creation in "shouting for joy."

Invitation to Group Sharing

1. What words of Jesus have staying power in my heart?

2. Do I know people who are feeling hopeless or defeated? How can I help them open up to the signs of God's care and concern around them?

3. What signs do I see in my life of hope and promise?

4. In what ways have I been dulled to the images of war, violence, disaster, or persecution? What can I do to shake off this dullness in order to become more alert and aware?

Invitation to Act

Determine a specific action (individual or group) that flows from your sharing. This should be your primary consideration. When choosing an individual action, determine what you will do and share it with the group. When choosing a group action, determine who will take responsibility for different aspects of the action. The following are secondary suggestions:

1. Name an organisation or institution you admire for being a sign of compassion and justice in our world. Think of a way to support or affirm the work its people are doing.

2. Make an active effort to keep yourself from becoming dulled by the media. Practice selective viewing over the next ten days, making very intentional choices about how much to watch and about your consumption of electronic and print media. Afterward, assess how these actions have affected your own sense of awareness and empathy for others.

Invitation to Closing Prayer

Give thanks to God (aloud or silently) for insights gained, for desires awakened, for directions clarified, for the gift of one another's openness and sensitivity. Conclude with the following:

Leader At the time of Jesus' first coming, before his birth, Zachary, father of John the Baptist, uttered these prophetic words.
Let us pray them now with a spirit of trust and hope as we await the coming again in glory of our Lord and Saviour, Jesus Christ.

Side 1 Blessed be the Lord, the God of Israel, for he has visited people, he has come to their rescue

Side 2 And he has raised up for us a power of salvation in the House of his servant David, even as he proclaimed, by the mouth of his holy prophets from ancient times, that he would save us from our enemies

Side 1 Thus he shows mercy to our ancestors, thus *he remembers* his holy *covenant*, the oath he swore to our father Abraham that he would grant us, free from fear to be delivered from the hands of our enemies, to serve him in holiness and virtue in his presence, all our days.

Side 2   And you, little child,
you shall be called Prophet of the Most High,
for you will go to the Lord
to prepare the way for him.
To give his people knowledge of salvation
through the forgiveness of their sins.

All   because of the tender mercy of our God
by which the daybreak from on high will visit us
to shine on those who sit in darkness and
death's shadow,
to guide our feet into the path of peace.

(Luke 1:68-79)

Last Sunday in Ordinary Time
Our Lord Jesus Christ the King

"My Kingdom Is Not of This World"

Invitation to Pray

Pause for a few moments of silence and enter more deeply into the presence of God.

> *Song:* "Hail, Redeemer, King Divine,"
> Patrick Brennan CSsR, Search Press

> *Proclaim the gospel:* John 18:33b-37
> Jesus before Pilate

Take a few minutes to savour a word, a phrase, a question, or a feeling that rises up in you. Reflect on this quietly or share it aloud. (The other Scripture readings of the day are Daniel 7:13-14 and Revelation 1:5-8.)

Invitation to Reflect on the Gospel

In this day and age, not many of us can attest to having much first-hand experience with kings. More pluralistic systems of governance have replaced sovereign ones and, even in some countries where rulers remain on the throne, their power is primarily symbolic. How, then, do we relate to this reading today?

Our imaginations, fuelled by books and films, conjure up stories of kings and queens of different ilk. Be they good or evil, wise or wanton, solicitous or cruel, we are aware of their power over others. Used well, it transforms kingdoms into Camelots where virtue and justice prevail, if only for a time. If abused, it bodes ill for all, throwing countries into chaos and even ruin.

In this passage from John's Gospel, Jesus stands up to Pilate's questioning with calm and conviction. He does not deny being "King of the Jews," but he rejects the idea that he is a political threat to Caesar or any other worldly power. "My kingdom does not belong to this world" (John 18:36), he says, noting that no army is on the march, readying for battle in order to free him. He states simply his purpose in coming into the world: "to testify to the truth" (John 18:37). This is achieved not through imposing his authority over others, but by an invitation into relationship. "Everyone who belongs to the truth listens to my voice" (John 18:37).

It is little wonder that those who have known the oppressive power of rulers and systems to enslave, entrap, and hold them "in their place" are the ones most open to this voice of Jesus. His words remind us that no one, not even a king, can withhold from us our rightful place in God's kingdom. It is there we each stand with equal dignity, cherished and beloved by the God who rules with justice and mercy.

The celebration of the feast of Christ the King falls each year on the final Sunday of the liturgical cycle. Next week the holy season of Advent begins, a time of celebration, expectation, and anticipation for the coming of Jesus Christ, the Alpha and the Omega, the beginning and the end. Rather than starting all over again, this movement into a new year continues our journey as a people who have been chosen as God's own. Together we look ahead, under Christ's leadership, to a time and a place foretold by the prophet of old.

"They shall beat their swords into ploughshares
        and their spears into pruning hooks;
One nation shall not raise sword against another,
        nor shall they train for war again" (Isaiah 2:4).

We set our sights anew to a kingdom built on the peace, the light, and the truth that is Jesus Christ, King of endless glory.

Invitation to Group Sharing

1. Name the traits that are found in a good and wise ruler. How do these help me better appreciate the kingship of Jesus Christ?

2. What does it mean to "belong to the truth" (John 18:37)? When do I find it hard to hold to the truth Jesus gives me?

3. How am I actively a sign of the reign of God in my home?
   in my place of work?
   in my parish?
   in the community at large?

4. What aspects of the reign of God can be seen in our midst today? How can I participate more fully in bringing this reign into fulfillment?

Invitation to Act

Determine a specific action (individual or group) that flows from your sharing. This should be your primary consideration. When choosing an individual action, determine what you will do and share it with the group. When choosing a group action, determine who will take responsibility for different aspects of the action. The following are secondary suggestions:

1. Determine what attitudes or actions you would like to embrace during the coming seasons of Advent and Christmas.

2. Decide how you will be a sign of God's reign in your family, in your place of work.

3. Make a list of how you relate to today's reading. What action response surfaces from your journaling? Act on this.

Invitation to Closing Prayer

Give thanks to God (aloud or silently) for insights gained, for desires awakened, for directions clarified, for the gift of one another's openness and sensitivity. Conclude with the following:

Leader   Let us collect our hopes, fears, wishes, and dreams
          for the fulfillment of the Kingship of Jesus Christ,
          and lift them in prayer to our God
          who hears and answers us.
          For the coming of a time of justice, especially for...

[Group members name, in a word or phrase, their special intentions.]

Leader   We pray to the Lord...

Response Lord, hear our prayer.

Leader   For the coming of a time of peace, especially for...

Leader   We pray to the Lord...R

Leader   For the coming of a time of mercy, especially for...

Leader   We pray to the Lord...R

Leader   God of justice, peace, and mercy,
We lift these prayers to you, in confident faith
that you will hear and answer them.
We pray this in the name of our Lord Jesus Christ,
who lives and reigns with you, forever and ever.

All   Amen

Music Resources

All of the music resources suggested in this publication can be found in common hymn books such as:

Laudate

Celebration Hymnal for Everyone

Gather

Hymns Old & New

Liturgical Calendar

Year B	2006		2009	
1st Sunday of Advent	Nov. 27, 2005		Nov. 30, 2008	
2nd Sunday of Advent	Dec.	4	Dec.	7
3rd Sunday of Advent	Dec.	11	Dec.	14
4th Sunday of Advent	Dec.	18	Dec.	21
Holy Family	Dec.	30	Dec.	28
Mary, Mother of God, Jan 1	Sunday		Thursday	
Epiphany	Jan. 8, 2006		Jan. 4, 2009	
Baptism of the Lord	Jan.	9	Jan.	11
2nd Sunday in Ordinary Time	Jan.	15	Jan.	18
3rd Sunday in Ordinary Time	Jan.	22	Jan.	25
4th Sunday in Ordinary Time	Jan.	29	Feb.	1
5th Sunday in Ordinary Time	Feb.	5	Feb.	8
6th Sunday in Ordinary Time	Feb.	12	Feb.	15
7th Sunday in Ordinary Time	Feb.	19	Feb.	22
8th Sunday in Ordinary Time	Feb.	26	---	---
1st Sunday of Lent	Mar.	5	Mar.	1
2nd Sunday of Lent	Mar.	12	Mar.	8
3rd Sunday of Lent	Mar.	19	Mar.	15
4th Sunday of Lent	Mar.	26	Mar.	22
5th Sunday of Lent	Apr.	2	Mar.	29
Palm Sunday	Apr.	9	Apr.	5
Easter	Apr.	16	Apr.	12
2nd Sunday of Easter	Apr.	23	Apr.	19
3rd Sunday of Easter	Apr.	30	Apr.	26
4th Sunday of Easter	May	7	May	3
5th Sunday of Easter	May	14	May	10
6th Sunday of Easter	May	21	May	17
Ascension +	May	25	May	21
7th Sunday of Easter	May	28	May	24
Pentecost	June	4	May	31
Trinity Sunday	June	11	June	7
Body and Blood of Christ	June	18	June	14

+ In many places, the Solemnity of the Ascension of the Lord is observed on the Seventh Sunday of Easter.

Liturgical Calendar

Year B			2006		2009	
9th Sunday in Ordinary Time	---	---	---	---	---	---
10th Sunday in Ordinary Time	---	---	---	---	---	---
11th Sunday in Ordinary Time	---	---	---	---	---	---
12th Sunday in Ordinary Time	---	---	June	25	June	21
13th Sunday in Ordinary Time	---	---	July	2	June	28
14th Sunday in Ordinary Time			July	9	July	5
15th Sunday in Ordinary Time			July	16	July	12
16th Sunday in Ordinary Time			July	23	July	19
17th Sunday in Ordinary Time			July	30	July	26
18th Sunday in Ordinary Time			---	---	Aug.	2
19th Sunday in Ordinary Time			Aug.	13	Aug.	9
20th Sunday in Ordinary Time			Aug.	20	Aug.	16
21st Sunday in Ordinary Time			Aug.	27	Aug.	23
22nd Sunday in Ordinary Time			Sept.	3	Aug.	30
23rd Sunday in Ordinary Time			Sept.	10	Sept.	6
24th Sunday in Ordinary Time	---	---	Sept.	17	Sept.	13
25th Sunday in Ordinary Time			Sept.	24	Sept.	20
26th Sunday in Ordinary Time			Oct.	1	Sept.	27
27th Sunday in Ordinary Time			Oct.	8	Oct.	4
28th Sunday in Ordinary Time			Oct.	15	Oct.	11
29th Sunday in Ordinary Time			Oct.	22	Oct.	18
30th Sunday in Ordinary Time			Oct.	29	Oct.	25
31st Sunday in Ordinary Time	---	---	Nov.	5	---	---
32nd Sunday in Ordinary Time	---	---	Nov.	12	Nov.	8
33rd Sunday in Ordinary Time			Nov.	19	Nov.	15
Christ the King			Nov.	26	Nov.	22

ORDERING INFORMATION
for
PRAYERTIME *Cycle A, B, C*

A Faith-Sharing book, for every group,
For every Sunday of the Year.
For both Small Christian Communities and other
church groups
£6.99 each – trade discount available for 5 copies or more

Available from:

The Diocesan Communications Office
Diocese of Westminster
Archbishop's House
Ambrosden Avenue
London
SW1P 1QJ

Tel: 020 7798 9000
Fax: 020 7798 9077

Email: enquries@rcdow.org.uk
Web: www.aywl.org.uk
        www.rcdow.org.uk

NOTES

NOTES

NOTES